Never Lick a Frozen Flagpole!

God has used Marvin's words to stir a healthy smile and a sigh in millions of us!

—Max Lucado, Author

When I came across the phrase "the sweet smell of encouragement" in this book, I thought of Marvin. His whole ministry has been devoted to building up instead of tearing down. *Never Lick a Frozen Flagpole!* is one more gift from a man who truly has the gift of encouragement.

—Mike Cope, Author and Minister, Highland Church, Abilene, Texas

Never Lick a Frozen Flagpole! is humorous, entertaining, upbeat, and positive in a God kind of way! Marvin helps us laugh at ourselves, love others, and enjoy life the way God meant it to be.

—Bob Willinger, Radio/TV Broadcaster

This book may be just the de-icer needed to thaw Christians frozen in discouragement and defeat. *Never Lick a Frozen Flagpole!* will warm the heart; anxieties will melt and threats will vanish. And then? Then you'll be free to breath easy again.

—Terry Rush, Author and Minister,
Memorial Drive Church, Tulsa, Oklahoma

There is nothing wrong with most readers that Marvin Phillips's stories and anecdotes won't fix! The book of Proverbs says "A cheerful heart is good medicine." Each chapter in this book is a fast-acting, power-packed, spiritual vitamin. Take one a day for the next 25 days, and you'll be ready to face the world and the devil himself!

—Victor Knowles, Author, *Please Pass the Pig*

This book is vintage Phillips. He pinpoints the foibles of life and God's solutions in a humorous and unforgettable way.

—Richard Rogers, Instructor, Sunset International Bible Institute

Marvin should have been named Barnabas. He writes like he talks—always upbeat, always enthusiastic. Reading this book is like sitting down for a short visit with Marvin. I always come away encouraged!

—Melvin Byrd, Director of Celebration, Seattle, Washington

Marvin Phillips has scored again! This collection of short, witty, practical modern-day parables is sure to be a hit. If you're reaching for ways to drive a lesson home, to spark your own creativity, or for some inspirational reading, *Never Lick a Frozen Flagpole!* is for you!

—Keith P. Keeran, Ph.D, President, Kentucky Christian College

In this new book, Phillips has concocted a spiritual milkshake of wisdom, biblical insight, humor, and down-to-earth practical tips for everyday living. This book motivated me to turn good intentions into action!

—Jimmy Sites, Senior Minister, Madison Church of Christ, Nashville, Tennessee

Things to think about, things to laugh about, things to pray about. Once again, Marvin Phillips has dipped his ladle into the well of stories, thoughts, and one-liners that make him such a great communicator. He is down-to-earth and right on the mark, and his lessons on life will make you grin till your cheeks hurt. If you don't feel better about life after reading this one . . . check your pulse.

—Jeff Walling, Author and Senior Minister, Providence Rd. Church

Never Lick a Frozen Flagpole!

More! Humorous Insights That Motivate and Encourage

MARVIN PHILLIPS

HOWARD BOOKS
A DIVISION OF SIMON & SCHUSTER
New York   London   Toronto   Sydney

Our purpose at Howard Books is to:

Increase faith in the hearts of growing Christians

Inspire holiness in the lives of believers

Instill hope in the hearts of struggling people everywhere

Because He s coming again!

HOWARD
BOOKS

Published by Howard Books, a division of Simon & Schuster, Inc.
1230 Avenue of the Americas, New York, NY 10020
www.howardpublishing.com

Never Lick a Frozen Flagpole! © 1999 by Marvin Phillips

Library of Congress Cataloging-in-Publication Data
Phillips, Marvin, 1931–
      Never lick a frozen flagpole! : more! humorous insights that motivate and encourage / Marvin Phillips.
            p.   cm.
      1. Christian life--Anecdotes. 2. Christian life--Churches of Christ authors. I. Title.
      BV4517.P38   1999
      248.4′02′07--dc21—dc21   98-56642
                                                                                    CIP

ISBN-13: 978-1-58229-009-6
ISBN-10:   1-58229-009-1

ISBN-13: 978-1-4165-3339-9
ISBN-10:   1-4165-3339-7

10 9 8 7 6

HOWARD and colophon are registered trademarks of Simon & Schuster, Inc.

Manufactured in the United States of America

For information regarding special discounts for bulk purchases, please contact: Simon & Schuster Special Sales at 1-800-456-6798 or business@simonandschuster.com.

Edited by Emily McMackin and Sue Ann Jones
Interior design by Vanessa Bearden
Illustrations by Kristen Myers

Scripture quotations not otherwise marked are from the New International Version, © 1973, 1978, 1984 by International Bible Society. Used by permission of Zondervan Bible Publishers. Other Scriptures quoted from THE MESSAGE *(MSG)*, © 1993, 1994, 1995, 1996. Used by permission of NavPress Publishing Group; the King James Version (KJV), © 1961 by The National Publishing Co.; the American Standard Edition of the Revised Version (ASV), © 1929 by International Council of Religious Education; the New King James Version © 1979, 1980, 1982, by Thomas Nelson, Inc.; The New Testament in Modern English (PHILLIPS), © 1958 by J. B. Phillips. All rights reserved. Italics in Scripture quotations were added by the author for emphasis.

In memory of

This book is dedicated to the memory of G. E. and Girt McElheny. They both died in 1997, past age ninety. They began watching my TV program while living in a retirement center in Tulsa. They attended *Peak of the Week Live!* as long as they were able to drive. G. E. was an avid reader. He often gave me books and shared ideas he thought would make good "Peak Lessons." Two of the chapters in this book are from his ideas: "Eye in the Sky" and "Get Out of the Kitchen." When I retired, they gave a substantial donation to get me started with Marvin Phillips Ministries, which continues to produce the TV series, *Peak of the Week Live!* They left a trust that continues to help fund the TV program and my trips to South Africa, which they enjoyed hearing about.

My life is considerably blessed and my ministry more effective because of their friendship, prayers, and financial support. It gives me great honor to dedicate this book to their memory!

> "Blessed are the dead who die in the Lord from now on." "Yes," says the Spirit, "they will rest from their labor, for their deeds will follow them."(Rev. 14:13)

Contents

CONTENTS

Preface

God has really been good to me. I was senior minister of a Tulsa church for twenty-six years. It grew from scratch to more than twelve hundred in Sunday attendance. I retired last year. I never intended to quit, just shift gears. Never in my wildest dreams could I have envisioned what God had planned for me.

Five things explain my exciting new ministry—Australia, South Africa, *Peak of the Week Live!,* trips and seminars, and ministry to the people where I live in Tulsa, Oklahoma.

The fun stuff includes regular trips to Australia, where my family lived for seven years. There are frequent trips to South Africa, where I've been going for the past ten years. We have formed Marvin Phillips Ministries, which produces the weekly TV series, *Peak of the Week Live!* I travel coast to coast speaking to churches, schools, and businesses. Perhaps the best part is that I still get to live in Tulsa. I get to minister to the people I have loved and worked with for the past twenty-seven years! It's the best of both worlds.

Never Lick a Frozen Flagpole! is a collection of my TV messages. These are all on *encouragement.* Come to think of it, most all my stuff is on encouragement.

Acknowledgments

I'm indebted to so many for the ideas behind these chapters.

To Randy Gill for that marvelous little "Don't Snap My Stick" story.

To Ben Mereness for the chapter title "The Four Beats of a Healthy Heart." Ben is really good at titles. I've used his ideas before and no doubt will again. To G. E. McElheny for his many ideas and constant encouragement to me. (See "In Memory Of" page!)

To Mark Crain for asking me to speak at Spring Training Youth Camp, 1997. That's where I did "It's How You Play the Game!"

To Marge Baker, longtime friend from San Antonio, Texas, for her words of encouragement and permission to use her idea on "Learn to Brake Before you Break!" She aspires to write a book along this line. You'll want to read it.

To Karen Bullock, from El Reno, Oklahoma, for sharing her marvelous story and essays from which I wrote "Life Is a Terminal Disease."

To Patsy Smith, from Arkansas, who sat next to me on the plane. From our conversation came the chapter on "How to Make a Difference!" There are beautiful people and terrific ideas everywhere you turn. That's what makes life so exciting.

I am honored that you are reading this, my sixth book. I hope you are *encouraged.* I hope your week is "peaked."

And don't forget, God loves you, and I love you, and that's the way it's gonna be!

Never Lick a Frozen Flagpole

Snow and ice covered the school grounds, but the sixth-grade class went outside for recess anyway. In Jean Shepherd's delightful tale called *A Christmas Story,* Ralph and Flick and Swartz and four or five other students huddled in the cold, their conversation creating clouds of vapor in their midst. Surveying the frosty schoolyard, one of the boys remembered a warning he'd heard from his father. If you touch your tongue to a frozen flagpole, his dad had said, you could never get it loose. You'd be there for life.

Another boy chimed in that his father actually knew a man who had touched his tongue to a frosty railroad track. The fire department had to come and get him loose.

"That's not so," said Flick, scoffing at his friends' stories.

CHAPTER ONE

All eyes darted from Flick to the school's frost-covered flagpole as Swartz, defending his father's integrity, hotly replied, "Then I dare you to do it!"

Daring is serious business to twelve-year-old boys.

Flick was tempted, but he didn't move. Then Swartz double-dared him. And as every twelve-year-old boy knows, it is almost impossible to withstand a double-dare. Only one thing is worse . . .

"I triple-dog dare you!" Swartz shouted.

That was it! No one could resist a triple-dog dare. Flick stuck out his tongue and headed for the flagpole. He really didn't want to do it. But how could he live with the guys if he backed down on a triple-dog dare? Throwing his chin up with a cocky air, he defiantly thrust his tongue against the frozen pole.

"Not so bad," he started to say. But the words wouldn't come out. And his tongue wouldn't come off the pole.

The bell rang. Recess was over, and the kids ran for their class-room. Flick, still attached to the flagpole, screamed bloody murder— as best he could.

Back in class, Miss Shields spotted the empty seat. "Where's Flick?" she asked.

No one could seem to remember just who Flick was. Finally she looked out the window. There stood poor little Flick with his tongue stuck fast to the flagpole. The fire department was hastily sum-moned. The police came, too, sirens screaming. The whole sixth-grade class watched from the window as the rescuers set the hapless boy free.

Flick returned to the classroom with his tongue bandaged. It would be at least a week before he could talk clearly.

Why Do We Lick the Frozen Flagpole?

We've all done stupid things. When we're twelve years old, it's often because of a dare. When we're adults, our moments of stupidity may arise from simple curiosity. Or risk-taking. Or yielding to some temptation even though we know better.

Many of us do stupid things because of our inherent sinful nature, that part of us the apostle Paul described in his letter to the Romans. We constantly fight against the pull of this nature to violate the law of the God in whose image we're made. When we lose the battle, we may find ourselves committing ridiculously foolhardy deeds or selfish and immoral acts.

But more often I believe it's our inherent curiosity, rather than our sinful nature, that makes us want to lick the frozen flagpole. After all, God created us with imagination and an adventurous spirit (some more adventurous than others!). And these parts of our makeup have nothing to do with evil. They're part of the marvelous zest for life we got at birth. And in these cases, licking that flagpole may seem stupid to others, but to us it's more like a lesson in life. We're curious. We try it. And we learn from the experience without killing ourselves or anyone else or losing too much blood.

Human curiosity is apparent from our earliest days on earth. Just think how youngsters are fascinated by a hot stove. Tell them, "No, don't touch. Hot!" and they stand staring at it in curious wonder, drawn by its strange appeal. *How hot?* they wonder. *Hot enough to melt my plastic horse? Hot enough to make the pages of my book turn black? Hot enough to . . .* They *want* to touch it.

Later the same youngsters wonder what will happen if they shove the tweezers in the electrical outlet. They watch *Superman* movies and wonder what it's like to fly. So they wrap a dishtowel around their necks, strip down to their Fruit of the Looms, and jump off the dining room table.

A few years later, as curious adolescents, they sneak out behind the barn and make cigarettes out of cedar bark wrapped in brown paper torn from a grocery sack. Or they somehow get possession of a cheap, fat cigar and light up. They don't want to become nicotine-addicted smokers. They're just curious, that's all. And the cigar isn't so bad at first. But ten minutes later, their stomachs are churning, and they're running for Mama.

Then kids grow up and wonder what it's like to jump out of an airplane, climb a mountain, or go scuba diving. They hitchhike around Europe or sail around the world. Sometimes curiosity leads folks to do things no one else can understand. They just seem like good ideas at the time. And later they give us memories that warm us and make us smile.

Here's an example: You might be surprised to learn that I own a Honda Gold Wing motorcycle. I'm no Hell's Angel, just a retired minister who enjoys roaring around curves doing fifty miles an hour at a forty-five degree angle, my hand on the throttle and the wind gliding over my helmet. It was curiosity that caused this glitch in my "normally normal" personality. I was thinking one day, *I've seen the world. I've seen a good bit of America. But I haven't seen my own state of Oklahoma.* So I got out a state map and drew a line around the perimeter of the state, following the back roads. Riding my motorcycle, I stayed off the interstates and purred through the towns, seeing the sights and meeting the people. I took four days and three nights and drove 1,496 miles. What an experience! Pretty tame, I guess, compared with licking a frozen flagpole. But for me, it was quite a thrill.

I traveled a couple of times with the venerable Dr. Norman Vincent Peale. He once told me, "Never think age! You'll either say, 'Oh, I'm too old for that' (in which case you'll miss out on a lot of life's good things), or you'll do all kinds of crazy things trying to look and act younger—and you'll end up looking like a fool."

The secret is to go with your spirit, he told me. Make the most of every day. Take a few chances now and then and put a little excitement and adventure in your life. When curiosity consumes you, go ahead. Lick the frozen flagpole if you must. It may hurt a little. But what fun you'll have later in the telling!

We are made in our Father's image; there is God in each of us (see Gen. 1:26). And that bit of immortality in our beings may be the source that sparks our curiosity, causing us to explore exciting new horizons in this marvelous world he created for us. Don't wait till all the lights are green! Get out there and live right now, while a couple of them are still flashing yellow. Take some chances. Grab some dreams. Go back (or more accurately, step forward) and get that degree you almost finished. Write that book that's been swirling around inside your head. Start your own business. Buy that sports car. Build that house. Take that dream vacation.

> That bit of immortality in our beings may be the source that sparks our curiosity.

If I had my life to live over, I'd spend my money and my lot differently. I'd own more toys, take more chances, step out on more adventures. I'd love more deeply and freely.

CHAPTER ONE

Put Some Excitement in Your Spiritual Life

I can't live my whole life over, but I can still live what's left of it with a joyful attitude of enthusiasm. One of the ways I can add zest and excitement to my everyday existence is to add some adventures to my walk with God. Our relationship with the Father can be a spiritual skydive, a true mountaintop experience. After all, one of the most exciting verses of Scripture says,

> Those who hope in the Lord will renew their strength.
> They will soar on wings like eagles;
> they will run and not grow weary,
> they will walk and not be faint. (Isa. 40:31)

My ministry has been an adventure! I began preaching at age seventeen. After serving a couple of churches in Texas and Arkansas, my family and I were called to Australia. Just imagine it! We left the States hardly knowing how we'd survive. But once we answered God's call, the money and the sponsoring church just fell into place. What a thrilling thing God's providence is!

Then, after seven years of this adventure in the "Land Down Under," we were called to help start a new church in Tulsa, Oklahoma, and we were there until I retired from that work after twenty-six years, eight months, and six days. We saw that congregation grow from ninety-one people to more than twelve hundred. Our highest attendance on a special day reached almost five thousand worshipers! We also began an annual International Soul-Winning Workshop that continues to this day, attracting more than twelve thousand people from all over the world to the Tulsa Fairgrounds for the yearly event.

Did I say I had retired? Well, don't think that means I've quit working! I'll never quit. God just transferred me to a different department. I now get to spend a month each year working in both Australia and South Africa. I do a weekly TV show, *Peak of the Week Live!* And I travel to churches and professional groups all over America participating in workshops and seminars.

Just God and Me

Through my work I've learned how exciting the spiritual life can be. It's just God and me, out there on the cutting edge, one curious adventure after another. Just as I once wondered, *What if we did a TV show, Lord? How could we do it? What would the format be?* I can now feel curiosity leading me into other adventures of spreading the Gospel.

I'm like the guy who said, "I used to endure my Christianity; now I'm enjoying it!" And another who said, "I'm having a lot more fun on my way to heaven than I ever did on my way to hell!"

You don't have to lick a frozen flagpole or respond to every triple-dog-dare that comes your way in order to live life with zest and enthusiasm. You don't have to skinny dip in the baptistry. But there *are* spiritual adventures out there, waiting to be experienced and enjoyed. There are people out there aching to be saved. And I know just the Guy to take along as your partner through the passage. He's got quite a history of adventures in his own right. And when it comes to loyalty, he'll love you like a Father.

Go on and live! Go with God.

2

Home Court Advantage

It is a foregone conclusion. Anyone with any sports knowledge understands it. Teams win better at home! It's true of any sport—football, basketball, baseball, anything. And it is true at any level—high school, college, or professional.

Now if there's one place where playing at home should not make a difference, it ought to be in professional sports. After all, these guys are pros! They're so good they are given multimillion-dollar contracts just to sign with the team. Except in play-off and championship games, the players get the same money whether they win or lose. So they should play at the same level no matter where, right?

Wrong!

Welcome to the NBA!

I picked up my copy of the *Tulsa World* one morning during the 1997 season and immediately flipped to the sports page. I scanned the standings in the National Basketball Association. The Chicago Bulls were on top, just as I had hoped. They were sixty-five and ten. The next closest team was thirteen-and-a-half games out.

And then I looked closer. I looked at the numbers in light of the home court advantage, and I noticed a startling piece of evidence that highlights the power of encouragement.

The NBA has two conferences (Eastern and Western) and four divisions (Atlantic, Central, Midwest, and Pacific). By the end of the season, each team had played an average of seventy-five games. Now stay with me as we look at an amazing phenomenon.

The top team (Chicago) had played seventy-five games and had a sixty-five/ten win/loss record. The worst team in the league (Vancouver Grizzlies) had played seventy-seven games and was 12 and 65.

Here's the intriguing part. When Chicago plays on the road, they win 75 percent of their games, but when they play in their home arena, they win a whopping 96 percent. In fact, their win/loss record at home is 37/1! On the other end of the spectrum, Vancouver wins only 11 percent of their games on the road but 20 percent at home.

It has nothing to do with the ability of the players. It has every-thing to do with the moral support of the hometown fans.

Of the twenty-nine teams in the NBA, only the Miami Heat has won more games on the road than at home. But the ratio is extremely close. They've won twenty-seven games at home and twenty-nine on the road. As you can see, when teams play before their home crowd, something happens. It has nothing to do with the ability of the players. It has everything to do with the moral support of the hometown fans.

What happens at these home games that makes the difference? Isn't it obvious? The home crowd offers loud, unwavering *encouragement!* Thousands of screaming, cheering fans paint their faces with team colors and wave giant hand signs declaring "We're number one!" They wear team jerseys and hold up banners for national TV. Cheerleading squads spend endless hours rehearsing and choreographing routines. All for the purpose of cheering on the home team. Even sports commentators are partial. During the heyday of the Chicago Bulls, even Shaquille O'Neal got no respect when he played in Chicago. But when it came time to announce the starting lineup for the home team, the lights went out, lasers blinked madly all over the arena, and a giant bull head appeared on the screen. The announcer screamed at the top of his voice, "And now your own Chicago Bulls!" Each word stretched into several seconds as he recited the names of Scottie Pippin, Luke Longley, and Ron Harper against the sound of frantic cheering. Even Dennis Rodman got deafening applause. And of course, they saved the best for last. "And starting at guard, Mi-i-i-i-chael Jordan!!!" And the Bulls went out there and won it for the home crowd!

Encouragement Wins the Game

Having folks around you to encourage you, to cheer you on, to believe in you, and to support you often makes the difference between winning and losing—even if you are outclassed and under-talented.

Having people surround us with love, praise, and encouragement has a profound effect on us. I give a speech to schools and churches called "Praise Your Kids into Greatness!" You can't drive your kids to excellence. If you try, they'll drive you to the grave. But if you praise them, believe in them, and support them, they'll break their backs trying to please you.

Try it in your church. We are such spectators in church. We pay the players to "do church" for us. And if they don't do a good job, we call for the umpire (elders, board) to get them "outta there!" Folks keep their preacher in hot water and wonder why he's hard-boiled. Try screaming your lungs out for your church leaders. Try praying for them and praising them. You can praise your church into greatness too!

Having close friends gives you a home court advantage. Jess Lair, a noted author from Montana, claims he has five close friends—the kind who would drop everything at a moment's notice and come to his aid if he needed them, the kind who would give him the shirts off their backs. Kenny Rogers sings, "She believes in me." We need friends who believe in us, friends who think we've got what it takes! We'll work ourselves to the bone for people who believe in us.

We often say, "It goes without saying!" That's the problem! A wife complains, "He never tells me he loves me." The husband responds, "She knows I love her. It goes without saying!" Yet the home court crowd is eager to say it. They scream, "We're number one!" They yell and cheer until the home team begins acting like the champions they believe them to be. Families need the home court advantage. Husbands, wives, children, and parents all need to learn how to be "cheerleaders" for their family.

Positive Reinforcement Packs Power

None of us plays well on the road. We need our hometown fans. We need people around us who believe in us and say so, loud and clear.

Not only does the team need the fans, they also need encourage-ment from each other!

Baseball is the only sport that uses the expression, "C'mon babe!" Roughly translated it means, "Come on, babe! I know you can do it!" Listen to the players encouraging each other. They give high-fives and pat each other on the backside to show their support. It spurs them on to do even better. One guy told me, "I've been patted on the back before. But it was too often, too hard, and too low!" I know the feeling!

Becoming a Spiritual Cheerleader

Make a conscious effort to become an encourager. Don't let a day go by without cheering someone up. When you see a newspaper clip-ping praising someone you know, cut it out and send it to him or her. Write across it, "I know this person. I'm proud of you!" Send cards. Give gifts. Express gratitude. Take the advice of a bumper sticker I once saw that said, "Do Random Acts of Kindness!" Lend a helping hand. Give someone a second chance. Forgive. Forgive again. And again. Keep doing it! Don't stop. Pick someone up. Make someone's day brighter! Visit a sick friend. Don't forget the forgotten. Smile at anyone who needs it. Everyone needs it!

The neat thing about cheering is that it does the "cheer-er" as much good as the "cheer-ee." That's the nature of encouragement. I have a special box filled with encouraging notes I've received through the years. It is my good-memories box. Many of the notes came at times when I needed them the most. That file has meant so much to me. Think how much notes of encouragement from you would mean to others. Pass the encouragement on!

The Bible is the handbook on the home court advantage! Jesus was an encourager. He didn't come to condemn, but to save (see John 3:17). The bad news is that you and I are sinners. The good news is that God still loves us and sees value in us. The Cross screams out the message that God thinks we're worth dying for. Early Christians were told to encourage one another (see 1 Thess. 5:11). The Bible pictures heaven as a grandstand where all those who've gone before us are cheering us on to victory (see Heb. 12:1).

You can choose to be a "builder" or a "wrecker." I'm choosing to be a hometown fan for you. I will encourage you to be an excellent Christian. It is the best way to live and the only way to die!

Cheer up! God's got a mansion in heaven with your name written on the mailbox. Don't miss it!

3

Don't Snap My Stick

He just sat there! A nine-year-old boy just sitting on a log by a campfire. Shoulders slumped, lips quivering, Chris fought to regain his composure as tears slipped down his cheek. He was heartbroken.

Chris was on vacation with his parents, Randy and LaJuana Gill, who were chaperoning a camping trip on Catalina Island for some teenagers from their youth group. As soon as they stepped foot on the island, Chris wandered away from the rest of the group to do his own thing.

Like any boy, Chris liked to explore, and there was plenty to explore on Catalina Island—rocks, streams, bugs—lots of stuff. Of all the prizes Chris found, he was most pleased with his discovery of "the stick." You know the one. Every boy searches for that special

CHAPTER THREE

stick. It has to be the right size and the right length. And this one was just right. Chris carved it with his pocketknife, honed it with rocks, and tempered it in the campfire. He was so proud of his stick. You'd almost have to be a nine-year-old boy to fully appreciate the significance of that stick.

However, his spirits were crushed when a teenage boy from the youth group reached over and broke off the end of his stick! Of course, the boy didn't know what he had done—to him, it was just a harmless prank.

But to Chris, it was a cruel attack. He slid off into the darkness and plopped down on a log. When his dad found him, he was just sitting there, his world broken by the thoughtless act. "What's wrong, son?" his dad asked. Chris felt the comfort of strong shoulders as his dad wrapped his arms around him; it was a place where he had often found refuge. Chris looked into his dad's face with tear-filled eyes and said, "He snapped my stick!"

I Know about Special Sticks!

Twice a year, I join a small group of men as we camp out in the Kiamichi Mountains in southeastern Oklahoma. When our sons reach age four, they can come on their first Kiamichi trip. It's like a rite of passage, an initiation into manhood. We camp in the wild on Black Fork Creek where there is no electricity, no cabins, and no running water. I always take my son-in-law, Dale, and my grandson, Kent, because it's such a marvelous time for us to bond with each other.

Kent knows about sticks. I've spent many afternoons helping him search for the right one, carving it to a point for him, and putting his initials on it. I've seen the look in his eyes as he proudly displayed it to his friends. He always insists on taking it home, and he guards it as a treasured possession.

The World Is Full of Stick Snappers

Some people snap your stick intentionally. They get a twisted satisfaction out of causing pain. They enjoy popping someone else's balloon, ruining someone else's party, or raining on someone else's parade!

Others don't mean to be stick snappers; they just don't know any better. They don't realize what special sticks mean to little boys and little girls, or big boys and big girls! But their thoughtless words and careless actions hurt just the same. As Christians, we must listen to the cries of struggling people who plead, "Don't snap my stick!"

We All Have Our Special Sticks

Some sticks are physical, like sandcastles on a beach that are carelessly trampled, tires on a new bike that are cruelly deflated, or a pretty new dress that is intentionally soiled.

As we get older, our search for special sticks sometimes moves beyond the physical. Trying out for the high-school football team can become your stick, and someone can snap it off by making fun of your efforts. Maybe you want to sing in the school choir, but someone puts you down when you don't make the cut or jokes about your sounding more like a crow than a nightingale! Perhaps you get up to speak before the class but hear giggling and whispering in the audience that make you feel as if someone just snapped your stick! Maybe you ask the prettiest girl in school for a date, and she says she wouldn't go out with you if you were the last boy on earth. The world is full of stick snappers!

CHAPTER THREE

Stick Snappers Come in Assorted Shapes and Sizes

You? With your past? From where *you* come from? You're going to do what? Parents, be aware that you can get into this act too. Do you tell your children that they always look a mess? Have you told them you're sorry you had them? Do you warn them that they'll end up in jail someday? Employers, do you say to an employee, "There's no way you could do that job!"? Do your friends sometimes snap your stick by mistaking your motives when you're trying to help? Some people snap your stick by saying, "You're putting on a little weight, aren't you?" or "That was a stupid thing to do!" There are even stick-snapping jokes! "Guys who are bald in front are the thinkers; guys who are bald in back are lovers! Those who are bald all over just *think* they are *lovers!*" Funny, right? Wrong! It's only funny when everyone is laughing. You have no right to have fun at another's expense. Find a better way to tell the same joke. For example, "Lace your fingers together. Those whose right thumb is over the left are the thinkers. Those with their left thumb on top are the lovers. Those with thumbs side by side just *think* they are *lovers!*" It's the same joke and just as funny, but no one is hurt. No one's stick is snapped!

What Is at Stake?

Just imagine what would've happened if Christopher Columbus had allowed the stick snappers to quench his exploring spirit. Just think what would have been lost if he'd listened to them when they said, "Hey Chris, that's a stupid idea. The world is flat. You'll get out there just so far and fall off the edge of the earth!"

Think about the Wright Brothers. Someone may have said, "Hey,

Orville! Wilbur! What're you making? If God had meant us to fly, he'd have put wings on us!" Do you realize we'd have no 747s today if someone had snapped the Wright Brothers' stick? And what about Beethoven who finished his last symphony after he had gone deaf or John F. Kennedy who made the outrageous claim, "We're gonna put a man on the moon!"? Stick snappers are everywhere; if we let them affect us, there wouldn't be anything worth getting excited about!

Marvin's Stick

Those who know me well can't believe I was ever bashful, but I was! In fact, I couldn't even read in front of my senior class. I was not trained to be a preacher. However, a preacher who was a "stick giver" and a "stick whittler" encouraged me. As a result, nine of us in our youth group became preachers. My church family could have laughed at my efforts to preach. Come to think of it, a lot of my efforts were pretty humorous. They could have reminded me of my lack of education, lack of confidence, or downright lack of ability! Fortunately, God held off the stick snappers until I was able to handle it. I went on to preach in one of the finest churches in America for twenty-six years, and now I get to travel from coast to coast and literally all over the world in missions and ministry.

Oh, the stick snappers came! In fact, they are still here. You need to know they never go away, but you can choose not to let them snap your stick!

God Made Us to Be Dreamers

We are all searching for our "special sticks." We are bursting with potential, ambitions, and aspirations. Within each one of us, there are dreams aching to get out!

And there are those who encourage us to reach for our dreams. Speakers, books, and tapes inspire us with messages that say, "You can do it! Find your stick! Dream your dream! Grab hold of life, and live it to the full."

These positive messages "scratch" on you. They invade your thinking and convince you to believe in yourself—you sense it and begin to listen. Before you know it, you let that positive radiance seep into your life—you begin to have dreams—then the dreams begin to have you! That's when great things start to happen.

You Can Trust Your Stick with God!

Because he relied on God, David believed he could defeat a giant. With this same faith, the great prophet Elijah won the victory at Mount Carmel when the odds were 850 to 1. God inspired Noah to build the only boat that would float when the flood came. He convinced Abraham that he would provide for him, and he did! The apostles turned the world upside down as they spread the Good News of Jesus. God doesn't snap sticks; he inspires dreams and grows heroes. Although these Bible characters lived among stick snappers, they were able to live out the dreams God put in their hearts because they trusted him. You can trust your dreams with God too. The Bible is loaded with stick-finding language. Some of it is captured in the following verses:

> God doesn't snap sticks; he inspires dreams and grows heroes.

And we know that in all things God works for the good of those who love him . . . If God is for us, who can be against us? (Rom. 8:28, 31)

Don't Snap My Stick

Let us not become weary in doing good, for at the proper time we will reap a harvest if we do not give up. (Gal. 6:9)

I can do everything through him who gives me strength. (Phil. 4:13)

Be faithful, even to the point of death, and I will give you the crown of life. (Rev. 2:10)

Along with you, I'm out there fantasizing, imagining, dreaming, and struggling for significance. I want you to love me, believe in me, forgive me, and encourage me, but please don't snap my stick!

Come before Winter

In a cold jail cell in Rome, an old man bends over a stone table with a quill in hand and an inkwell nearby. Decades of love and memories go into the few words, which will eventually form the sixteenth book of the New Testament. The aged apostle Paul writes, "Do your best to get here quickly. All my friends who were with me are gone. One because of the pull of the world, and others because they had business in other places. I am alone! Oh, and when you come, could you please bring my books and notes?" (2 Tim. 4:9–13, paraphrase).

Paul will die in that jail cell, but he will die learning and studying the Word of God to the end. As a sudden chill pierces his frail body, he adds, "And bring my coat that I left in Troas!" (2 Tim. 4:13, paraphrase).

It's easy to infer from these passages that Paul is lonely! He writes, "At my first trial no one was there to defend me. They have all forsaken me. I pray that it may not be held against them!" (2 Tim. 4:16, paraphrase).

During this time, Paul remembers Jesus, who was abandoned by his closest friends when he suffered alone in the Garden of Gethsemane. Paul knows the feeling. But he handles the pain of desertion with the same remarkable grace and poise as the Son of God.

He continues to write, "But the Lord stood by my side. He gave me strength so that I could keep preaching even though I am in jail. I think, no, I pray that I can keep preaching for a little while longer. But winter is coming. No ships will be sailing again until spring. I don't know what is going to happen, so could you hurry? Try to get here before winter! After then, I fear it will be too late! I remember your tears at our last parting. I'd like to look upon your face one last time" (2 Tim. 4:17–21, paraphrase).

The Writer

The story of Paul takes your mind back to chapters 7–9 of the book of Acts. Paul starts out as Saul the persecutor, a strict Pharisee who believes that Jesus is a fake. We get our first glimpse of Saul as he offers his support to the angry mob stoning Stephen. Saul is a participant in the execution of one of the first Christian martyrs.

But something amazing happens while Saul is on a road trip to kill Christians. Jesus Christ appears to him on the Damascus road, and he is converted. In Damascus, Ananias preaches to Saul and baptizes him into Christ, and Saul, soon to be renamed Paul, begins to preach the Christ he once opposed!

Three missionary journeys soon follow. On the second one, he picks up Timothy as an intern. Timothy's mother is Jewish and his father Greek, and Paul sees him as a capable apprentice—one who will carry on his mission once he is no longer able. That day comes sooner than Paul anticipates! Paul is arrested and jailed in Jerusalem. He also spends time in jail in Caesarea and finally in Rome.

Second Timothy is probably the last book Paul wrote, and it's a tearjerker. He composed it from a lonely prison cell in Rome. By that time, Timothy and Paul had become close; they were like father and son. It reminds me of the bond between the Lord Jesus and his Father! Paul probably had more to do with Timothy's upbringing than any other male. It is a beautiful last letter from father to son.

The Plea

I was once urged by Dave Wardell, cofounder of Promise Keepers, to read 2 Timothy all the way through, every day for thirty days! I read it from a different translation every day and have been in love with the book ever since. Not only is it filled with emotional and spiritual instruction and advice, but it challenges us to give our best to the Lord who gave us his best!

Paul's plea, "Come before winter," haunts me! Paul has encountered the threat of death many times during his service to Jesus Christ—and he isn't afraid to die—but he would like just one more visit from Timothy before he goes to be with the Lord.

It's almost winter, and soon the ships will not be able to leave port—it's simply too dangerous. More than once, ships have tried to beat nature, only to end up at the bottom of the sea. Paul has been in three shipwrecks himself and has spent more than one day and night in the deep. He knows that if Timothy is to come, it must be *now*. He urges him to do so before the opportunity passes by.

We will never know whether Timothy made it or not. Did Paul go friendless to the grave, or did Timothy stand by his side as he was beheaded for the cause of Christ? We do know, however, that time is running out for all of us. As William Golden writes in one of his hymns, "Life's evening sun is sinking low; a few more days and I must go!"

Now Is the Time!

When kids leave home for college, they tell their parents, "Don't worry. I'll write!" Yet they get busy and forget. Our grandparents and parents age in front of our eyes. We plan to spend more time with them, often saying to ourselves, "I must get over to see them soon." But time is swift and cruel. Before we know it, they are gone, and we are left with good intentions.

Paul Harvey spoke of attending his mother's funeral. His position and prosperity had allowed him to do lots of nice things for her. "But," he said, "I didn't do the little things." How she would have appreciated an occasional call, a little remembrance, or a few more hugs and kisses.

It reminds me of the poem "Around the Corner" by Henson Towne.

> Around the corner I have a friend,
> In this great city that has no end.
> Yet the days go by and weeks rush on,
> And before I know it, a year is gone.
> And I never see my old friend's face,
> For life is a swift and terrible race.
> He knows I like him just as well,

Come before Winter

As in the days when I rang his bell,
And he rang mine; we were younger then,
And now we are busy, tired men.
Tired with playing a foolish game.
Tired with trying to make a name.
"Tomorrow," I say, "I will call on Jim,
Just to show that I'm thinking of him."
But tomorrow comes and tomorrow goes,
And distance between us grows and grows.
Around the corner, yet miles away,
"Here's a telegram, sir"—
Jim died today.
And that's what we get and deserve in the end.
Around the corner, a vanished friend.

Parents, seize opportunities to spend time with your kids. Erma Bombeck once told a story about a boy named Mike. When he was three, he wanted a sandbox. His dad said, "It'll kill the grass!" and his mom said, "The grass will grow back!" When Mike was five, he wanted a jungle gym in the backyard, but his dad said, "We'll have kids all over the place. They'll tear everything up, and the grass will die for sure!" But Mike's mom said, "It will grow back!" Later on, he wanted to have a campout in the backyard. Then he asked for a basketball goal. And so it went. Mike's dad worried about the grass, but Mike's mom always said, "It will grow back!"

Then one summer, the lawn was neatly cut, hedged, and manicured. But Mike's dad never saw it. Instead, he stared out into the lawn with lonely eyes and asked, "He will come back, won't he?"

So go life's cycles. The spring of hope gives way to the summer of opportunity. Summer slips into the fall of passing chance. Winter comes all too soon, and it's too late to say "I'm sorry," "I love you," or "Please forgive me."

Now is the time for you to seize your opportunities. Repent of that sin you are harboring. Start back to church and commit your life to Jesus. An old hymn by William Kirkpatrick says it well: "I've wandered far away from God. Now I'm coming home!" But hurry, winter is coming!

Did Timothy Make It?

Suppose Timothy was like us? He meant to go, but something always came up. Perhaps he finally determines to go, but when he goes down to the dock to catch the next ship to Rome, he discovers that it is too late. Winter has already set in! The ships have pulled into the dry dock for protection from the coming inclement weather.

Immediately, panic begins to seize Timothy as he tells the captain, "I want passage on the first ship of spring! I've got to get to Rome, you see. My mentor is there. He's my dear father and friend!"

Maybe he does sail on the first ship, but he has lost four long months. He strains every mile of the trip, as if his anticipation can make the ship go faster. Finally, he reaches Rome! He gets directions to the Caesar Correctional Center. He races down the hall to Paul's cell and tells the jailer, "I want to see Paul! I'm his son, Timothy!"

Winter comes all too soon, and it's too late to say "I'm sorry," "I love you," or "Please forgive me."

"Oh, yes! Paul spoke of you often," the jailer says. "He said you were like a son to him! He was executed last month. His last words were to tell you he loved you!"

Come before Winter

Timothy turns away from the scene as tears scald his eyes! *Why didn't I come sooner?* he wonders.

I want to believe Timothy made it to see Paul before he died. But whether he did or not, Paul's cry, "Come before winter," speaks to us today. Our fault is not that we want to do wrong. We have good intentions! We mean to get around to it, but winter comes too quickly for many.

You can avoid having regrets by living in the now. Realize the value of time, and be aware that it is slipping away at a tremendous speed. Live life for today; do what ought to be done. "Do thy diligence to come before winter!" (2 Tim. 4:21 KJV).

5

The Four Beats of a Healthy Heart

I had all sorts of bad symptoms—shortness of breath, lack of energy, and bouncing blood pressure. My doctor said, "We'll put you in the hospital and run some tests." That was the last thing I wanted to hear. I couldn't prove it, but I really believed there were ghouls down in the bowels of the hospital asking, "What can we stick into him? How far into him can we stick it? How much can we draw out of him?" Well, they did all those things and more. Then the doctor came in with a two-inch stack of papers bearing my results. It was more than I ever wanted to know about myself. "I have good news and bad news," the doctor said. "The good news is that there is nothing organically wrong with you! The bad news is that you have an occupational hazard called job-related stress syndrome!"

Oh, boy, and me a preacher! Every Sunday I preached about peace, love, joy, and serenity, yet my body and lifestyle made people afraid to "catch" what I had!

I ventured on a quest to find out how to improve my lifestyle. Fifteen years after that traumatic episode in my life, I know the answer—fitness and attitude! Actually, I have discovered that there are four things that lead to better health. I will refer to them as the four beats of a healthy heart.

Balance Is the Key

Balance is essential for developing a healthy heart! Some people believe the body is everything. They don't waste their time reading books or educating themselves! Instead, they join health clubs, pump iron, and get plenty of exercise. Others devote hours to cultivating their mind. They read everything they can get their hands on and sometimes neglect their bodies while staying in school all their lives. One philosophy produces a musclebound idiot; the other, an academic bookworm.

What would a person look like if he developed only one arm? What would happen to a field-goal kicker if he neglected every other part of his body except the leg and foot that he uses to kick extra points? Or suppose a guy with 20/20 eyesight decided to cover one good eye and save it until his sight started to go in the other. Would he uncover an eye with perfect sight or would it have already gone bad due to lack of use? Balance is the key! So we're back to the four beats of a healthy heart! Hop on the treadmill. Let's see how you do!

Beat Number One Is Nutrition

Good health is normal and intended. The universe lends itself to it. Seasons, sunshine, rain, plants, water, and trees all cooperate to enhance our health. Nature holds the powers of healing and recovery, but we must cooperate by taking care of our bodies.

Americans often dig their graves with their teeth. Too much of our eating is "face entertainment." We don't eat what's good for us; we eat what smells, looks, and tastes good! What we eat and the amount we take in are extremely important. You become what you eat! Now, this may be discouraging to a guy eating a turkey sandwich.

> Good health is normal and intended. The universe lends itself to it.

Motivational speaker Ed Foreman once offered a humorous but accurate description of an average American's day. You start by oversleeping and waking up with precious little time to get to work. You grab a quick cup of coffee and a greasy doughnut on your way out the door. By midmorning, you are empty. So when your stomach cries out for food, you gulp down another cup of coffee, heavily laced with sugar, and another greasy doughnut. You make it to lunch, but deadlines are pressing. So you choke down a bowl of chili, sprinkled with corn chips, and another cup of strong, black coffee before getting back to work.

That night you eat your favorite meal—a thick, juicy steak, a baked potato loaded with sour cream, and a salad smothered in high-calorie dressing. Before long, you're full! You can still chew, but you can't swallow. But wait, surely you can make room for dessert. After a few slices of pie, you waddle over to the couch and plop down. "Honey, bring in the buttered popcorn and a pop," you casually say as you turn on a late-night movie. You wake up in your chair at 2:00 A.M. and drag your tired body off to bed. The next morning you oversleep again, and all you have time for is a cup of coffee and a doughnut. Wait, doesn't this sound familiar?

Consider the following three rules for better nutrition.

1. Eat the Right Stuff

Cut back on fat, fast food, fried food, and red meat! I once attended a Peter Lowe seminar at which someone spoke on "Ten Foods You Should Never Eat!" His taboo list included processed meats, fast food, Equal, alcohol, mayonnaise, and dairy products. He told us, "Fish is better than fowl, and fowl is better than mammal." He also urged us to eat lots of fresh fruits and vegetables.

Great advice, even though it's not the American way! By following these suggestions, my cholesterol dropped from 248 to 181.

2. Eat Less

Eat until you're satisfied, not until you're full. If you were brought up like me, you belonged to the Clean Your Plate Club and were taught that cooks like it better when you eat a lot, ask for more, and save room for dessert. This philosophy reminds me of the Irish comedian Hal Roach's description of how the Irish get you to drink more. They say, "Have another one. Here, get this down you. Come on now, drink it down!" But when you're bent over the sink the next morning, they're saying, "Come on now, get it up!"

3. No Second Helpings or Late-Night Snacks

Americans are famous for their snacks. Who can watch a football game, especially the Super Bowl, without a table full of pretzels and popcorn? And the danger is that with all that watching, you aren't even aware of how much you're eating!

Beat Number Two Is Exercise

Americans are dying from a sedentary lifestyle. We handle stress by sitting still and watching TV. If we want to exercise, we watch an exercise video!

Aerobics has become extremely important in my life. It's helpful to distinguish between aerobics, anaerobics, and isotonics. Anaerobics is stop-and-start exercise, like tennis, baseball, and walking at work. Isotonics involves resisting a movement one way by pushing against it the opposite way. Aerobics is continuous exercise that gets your heart rate up to a certain percentage of its maximum and holds it there. Aerobics has a "Roto-Rooter" effect on your arteries. It helps keep your arteries from becoming clogged and blocked, and it reduces the risk of a heart attack by 60 percent. It also promotes stronger blood circulation to the brain, which in turn produces more energy and creativity. To get all these benefits, you need to participate in some sort of aerobic activity. It should be done three to four times a week for twenty minutes at a time.

I get my aerobic exercise by jogging, and I have found that it is important to make the decision to jog the night before! If you wait until morning to decide, you'll sleep in. I always ask myself after I run, "Are you glad you did?" The answer is always yes! I can't say I always enjoy jogging, but I enjoy the benefits it brings.

By the way, rest is also an essential part of your exercise program!

As Jesus said, "Come with me by yourselves to a quiet place and get some rest" (Mark 6:31).

Beat Number Three Is Attitude

It is so important to have a positive attitude! Stress is fatal to negative thinkers. Like Zig Ziglar says, "Attitude, more than aptitude, determines altitude!" You can choose to be a positive thinker! In my *Peak of the Week Live!* TV show, I have my audience stand and repeat the following phrases:

> I'm made in God's image!
> I can choose my attitude!
> I choose to feel great!

All of these statements are true. God *did* make us in his image (see Gen. 1:26). Attitude *is* a choice—and we always have a choice. And we *can* choose to feel great anytime we want; outward circumstances have nothing to do with it. It all depends on the choices we make!

The Bible says, "As [a man] thinks in his heart, so is he" (Prov. 23:7 NKJV). You can be easily influenced by what you think and what you read. Therefore, you must choose carefully what you put into your mind.

Years ago, the highways were dirt, and the ruts would get very deep in the rainy season. At the beginning of a long stretch of muddy road was a sign that said, "Choose your ruts carefully. You'll be in them for the next twenty miles!" Likewise, you must choose your thoughts and attitudes carefully. Look on the bright side, and believe in the outcome. What you're thinking right now could be determining the course of your entire life—maybe even your eternity!

Beat Number Four Is Spirituality

Here's the tricky one! Spirituality simply refers to a close relationship with God. Now, I'm not trying to sneak up behind you with a sermon. It's just that we all have a "hidden hunger" that can only be filled by God. We understand physical hunger. Babies naturally take to their mothers' breasts. Feeding them is the only way to satisfy their cries at night. We don't lose this instinct as we get older. We can choose not to eat, but we can't ignore our pangs of hunger.

In light of this fact, is spiritual hunger so hard for us to understand? I once heard a story about two young boys who captured an eagle and put it in a cage. They gave it plenty of food and water, but it was no use. The eagle sat in the cage with folded wings and sad eyes, refusing to eat. It was dying! And why? The eagle wasn't created for a caged existence. It was created to soar to the heights of heaven, to nest on the edge of a cliff, and to be lifted into the sky on the winds of the storm. It couldn't exist in a cage.

Similarly, man wasn't created for a caged or restricted lifestyle either. Humans are the only creatures in the universe who are made in God's image, and nothing less than a godlike lifestyle will satisfy. Man was made for a relationship with his Creator; we all have a hunger for God! As Jesus said, "Apart from me you can do nothing" (John 15:5).

All of us know that food is the only thing that will satisfy our physical hunger; we should also recognize that God alone can satisfy our spiritual hunger.

Take a Heart Check

Each year I get a thorough physical. The doctors always take an electrocardiogram, which tells them the condition of my heart. I suggest that you take a different type of electrocardiogram: Check yourself for these four beats of a healthy heart—nutrition, exercise, attitude, and spirituality. You and I need these four beats to have a healthy heart and a successful life, just as a table needs all four legs to keep from spilling its contents onto the floor or just as a horse needs all four legs in order to carry its load. Don't go through life staggering when you could be soaring!

The Eye in the Sky

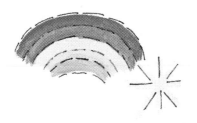

G. E. and Girt McElheny were great friends of mine. I visited them every week at Kaiser Health Care Center in Tulsa, Oklahoma. They both died recently; G. E. was ninety-one-years old and Girt was ninety-three. They began watching my TV show, *Peak of the Week Live!,* as residents of Methodist Manor House. (I'm told that I'm a big hit with the nursing-home crowd). They attended the live class when I taped it every Wednesday night at Garnett Church of Christ. They continued to be regular viewers until they were no longer able to attend.

G. E. always gave me books and articles he thought would help with my ministry. He often had ideas he thought would make good lessons for *Peak of the Week Live!* This is one of his!

CHAPTER SIX

There's an All-Seeing Eye Watching You!

Years ago, in a small country church in Texas, we used to sing a song called, "There's an All-Seeing Eye Watching You!" Part of it goes like this,

> All along on the road,
> To the soul's true abode,
> There's an eye watching you!
> Every step that you take,
> His great eye is awake!
> There's an eye watching you!

In Psalm 139, David says that God knows all about us. He knows us inside and out. He knows every move we make and our words before we speak them. David asks, "Where can I go from your Spirit?" (v. 7). The fact that anyone would *want* to escape God's presence shows that he or she doesn't really understand God. What does the Bible say about this "eye in the sky"? "If I go up to the heavens, you are there; if I make my bed in the depths, you are is there!" (v. 8).

I know! I'll get up early—get a head start. I'll board a jet airplane and travel to the furthest point on the globe. "Even there your hand will guide me, your right hand will hold me fast!" (v. 10).

I know what I'll do. I'll wait till it's dark. Surely God can't see what I'm doing or what I'm about to do in pitch-blackness. But, "even the darkness will not be dark to you; the night will shine like the day, for darkness is as light to you" (v. 12).

God knew us even before we were born. Wow! Those who favor abortion ought to think long and hard about these verses:

For you created my inmost being, you knit me together in my mother's womb. . . . When I was woven together in the depths of the earth, your eyes saw my unformed body. All the days ordained for me were written in your book before one of them came to be. . . . When I awake, I am still with you. (vv. 13, 15–16, 18)

The Eye in the Sky Sees Everything

There's no question about it, God knows everything about us: "Knowing their thoughts, Jesus said, 'Why do you entertain evil thoughts in your hearts?' " (Matt. 9:4). Then in the book of Hebrews we read, "Nothing in all creation is hidden from God's sight. Everything is uncovered and laid bare before the eyes of him to whom we must give account" (Heb. 4:13).

That verse used to scare me. My mother used it to help me be a good boy. She'd say, "When you're out there in the dark, God sees you. When you are away from home, God knows what you're doing. If you crawl into the backseat of a car with some girl, God knows what you're doing back there!" The thought terrified me!

I visited a church that had a picture of a huge eyeball hanging over the baptistery. It glared at the audience as they sang, "There's an all-seeing eye watching you." The eye is there, and someday we must give an account to God for every careless word we've spoken (see Matt. 12:36).

What Kind of Eye Is It?

It's not a blind eye! It doesn't wink at rebellion or excuse sin. "For the eyes of the Lord are on the righteous and his ears are attentive to their prayer, but the face of the Lord is against those who do evil" (1 Pet. 3:12).

It's not a spying eye, a critical eye, or a vengeful eye!

It's an Understanding Eye

Have you ever been misunderstood? I visited with a young lady who was dying from cancer. Not only had the disease ravaged her body, but it had also affected her attitude. She had abandoned her loving nature and become carping and critical. She even told me, "Isn't it horrible what sin can do to your attitude?" Then she read me one of her favorite verses: "The Spirit helps us in our weakness. We do not know what we ought to pray for, but the Spirit himself intercedes for us with groans that words cannot express" (Rom. 8:26).

In the margin next to that beautiful verse, she had written, "God has never misunderstood you!"

It's comforting to know someone really understands. God does; the eye in the sky understands!

It's a Caring Eye

We often wonder, "Who really cares about me?" Sometimes it seems like no one does! But the all-seeing eye cares! "Cast all your anxiety on him because he cares for you" (1 Pet. 5:7).

The autobiography of Jesus can be summed up in three words—vision, emotion, and action! He saw the crowds, had compassion on them, and taught in their towns and villages (see Matt. 9:35–38). Jesus saw—he *really* saw! And he cared—he *really* cared. His life was backed with actions that proved it.

I like the lyrics to "Does Jesus Care?" written by Frank E. Graeff.

The Eye in the Sky

Does Jesus care when my heart is pained
Too deeply for mirth and song;
As the burdens press, and the cares distress,
And the way grows dreary and long?

Does Jesus care when I've said good-bye
To the dearest on earth to me,
And my sad heart aches till it nearly breaks
Is it aught to Him? Does He see?

O yes, He cares; I know He cares,
His heart is touched with my grief;
When the days are weary,
The long nights dreary,
I know my Savior cares.

Jesus cares when you're hurting, when you're tempted, when you've lost loved ones, when you don't know what to do, and when you feel lost—too lost to be found and too unworthy to be saved. Isn't it wonderful to know Jesus still cares?

It's comforting to know someone really understands. God does; the eye in the sky understands!

It's a Loving Eye

The Bible contains thousands of scriptures about God's love for us.

Romans 5:6–8 says it best: "You see, at just the right time, when we were still powerless, Christ died for the ungodly. Very rarely will anyone die for a righteous man, though for a good man someone might possibly dare to die. But God demonstrates his own love for us in this: While we were still sinners, Christ died for us."

CHAPTER SIX

The One who knows you best, loves you most! Jesus knows all about you. You've never fooled him a day in your life. He sees every deed, hears every word, and knows every motive behind what you've done. Yet knowing what he knows, he still thinks you're worth dying for. And it's a humbling thing to be died for!

No wonder John 3:16 is called the "golden text" of the Bible. "For God so loved the world that he gave his one and only Son, that whoever believes in him shall not perish but have eternal life."

The Cross argues your worth. Have you ever felt too ugly to be loved or too sinful to be saved? It is the greatest feeling in the world to know someone really loves you, and you can be sure the Eye in the Sky does!

It's a Cheering Eye

The crowd couldn't understand why Jesus associated with sinners, so he gave them two word pictures. In Luke 15, he proclaimed the Good News of God in a nutshell. He tells a story about a shepherd who had a hundred sheep, and one got lost. He left the ninety-nine safely in the fold and went out to search for the lost sheep. He searched until he found it, put it on his shoulders, and brought it home. He called his neighbors and threw a party. Jesus said, "That's the way it is with God when one sinner repents." He added that "there is rejoicing in the presence of the angels of God over one sinner who repents" (v. 10). When the prodigal son came home, his father gave a banquet in his honor. The father rejoiced, saying, "My son was lost and is found; he was dead and is alive!" Like he told the older brother, "We *had* to celebrate." (see v. 32).

Hebrews 12 pictures Bible heroes of ages past sitting in the heavenly grandstand and cheering us on! They want us to win! They know how it feels to be tired. They've been there too. They also know that with God's help, you can go on. You can make it. So they cheer! We should listen to them and to God! And from somewhere deep within, we will find the courage to suck it up and go on to victory.

Do you ever get the idea there are those who like to see you fail? It is helpful to know that those who really count want you to win. You've got no enemies "over there." The heavenly grandstand cheers you on, and Jesus is the head cheerleader. Thank God for the all-seeing eye! Keep watching over us!

It's How You Play the Game

When I was invited to speak about "The Rules of the Game" at a spring training camp, I pulled out that great sports-rule reference book: the Bible.

Are you surprised to hear that a retired minister was invited to speak at spring training? Or that the Bible talks a lot about sports? That's what I asked my audience at the camp—actually a retreat organized by Mark Crain, youth minister at the church where I had served as senior minister for more than twenty-six years. He had invited me to speak to the young people gathered at Dry Gulch Camp near Pryor, Oklahoma, for a retreat focused on the spring-training theme. All the sessions were aimed at youth and centered on sports-related topics with titles such as "Let's Play Ball!" "Runner,

Take Your Base!" and "Tagging Up!"

While my session was billed as "The Rules of the Game," Mark said I didn't have to talk about the rules necessarily but on "the way the game is played."

That's when I pulled out my Bible and turned to the advice of that great Christian coach, the apostle Paul. He often compared the Christian life with racing, wrestling, and boxing. For example, he said:

> You've all been to the stadium and seen the athletes race. Everyone runs; one wins. Run to win. All good athletes train hard. They do it for a gold medal that tarnishes and fades. You're after one that's gold eternally. I don't know about you, but I'm running hard for the finish line. I'm giving it everything I've got. No sloppy living for me! I'm staying alert and in top condition. I'm not going to get caught napping, telling everyone else all about it and then missing out myself. (1 Cor. 9:24–27 MSG)

And he warned:

> We wrestle not against flesh and blood, but against principalities . . . against spiritual wickedness in high places. (Eph. 6:12 KJV)

Then he summed it up quite simply:

> An athlete who refuses to play by the rules will never get anywhere. (2 Tim. 2:5 MSG)

Athletes understand Paul's coaching advice. They know spring training isn't always fun. It's a lot of work: grueling repetition, sore muscles, aching feet, total exhaustion. But every day the contenders are out there, giving it all they've got. They run laps. They lift weights. They run the plays, practice the steps, refine their movements. Then they do it again. And again.

How do they do it? What keeps them going when exhaustion sets in and pain threatens to overwhelm them? It's the picture they hold in their minds of themselves winning the trophy. A Super Bowl ring. A gold medal. A World Series Title.

How to Be a Champion

Athletes learn a lot of lessons on their way to becoming champions. Here are a few of them, gleaned from the Golden Rule Book.

Give Your Best

You've watched the Dallas Cowboys, right? Each player gives his best every minute of every game. You may say, "I've seen times when Troy Aikman didn't give his best."

Now, you may have seen Aikman throw interceptions and get sacked on an off day, but he was still giving the best he could give in that specific game. They all do—Michael Jordan in basketball, Pete Sampras and Martina Hingas in tennis, Tiger Woods in golf. They don't always win, but they always give their best.

Maybe you think these sports superstars play hard because they are paid the big bucks. Perhaps you say, "Pay me a million dollars, and I'll give my best too!" But to real champions, the money isn't the important thing. These athletes have consistently given each game their best effort since the days when no one even came to see them compete, let alone *paid* to see them play!

I watched the Special Olympics a few years ago. Thirty-five

hundred disabled kids were playing their hearts out, giving their best. The three-meter diving contest was won by a young girl who had to be helped from her wheelchair to the board. A twelve-year-old boy won the hundred-meter dash even though he didn't even run in a straight line. These little champions showed the same spirit as those sports celebrities making the big bucks. They weren't perfect, but they were giving their best effort.

Set Goals

In sports, it's pretty obvious what the game's goal is, and everyone knows when one is achieved. But just in case the audience missed it, sometimes the scorer puts on a little extra show to please the crowd. In football, for example, when a player crosses the goal

line and earns six points for his team, he sometimes celebrates in the end zone with strange jumps, gestures, and gyrations. Watching some of these antics, I'm reminded of the story about the two dogs who were watching a football game. When they saw one guy jumping and dancing exuberantly in the end zone, one of them commented, "If we moved like that, they'd worm us!"

In most competitions, there's more than one chance to score a goal. Victory is achieved as the goals accumulate inning by inning, set by set. A football team gets four downs, or chances, to move the ball ten yards. If they make it, they are rewarded with four more downs to move the ball ten more yards or score a touchdown. This kind of incentive is called an SRO (short-range objective), a reward for doing good and motivation to do better.

It's How You Play the Game

Talking about short-range objectives reminds me of the two rich guys from Texas who hunted elk every year in Canada on the same lake. They usually had the same pilot-guide fly them to their favorite campsite. This year they ended up with a different pilot-guide. They got out their maps and showed him exactly where they wanted to go.

"You're crazy," he said. "I know that place. The lake is too short. The trees are too tall. I could never get you in there!"

"That's funny," the two hunters said. "We go to that exact spot every year. Our regular pilot had a plane about like yours. He always got us in there!"

Well, it got to the other pilot's pride. "Get in the plane," he barked. He put the two hunters and their gear in the plane and took off. With great expertise he made his way down through the trees, onto the lake, and up to the dock. As he unloaded their gear, they said, "Come back for us in four days!"

In four days he was back. With the same expertise he came down through the trees, hit the lake perfectly, and pulled up to the dock. There were the two hunters with their gear and three large elk.

The pilot said, "You're out of your mind if you think I can get you and your gear and these elk all on my plane and get out of here!"

They said, "We got three elk last year!"

"Get in the plane!" the pilot snapped. He strapped one elk to each pontoon and the third over the tail of the plane. He put the men and their gear inside, taxied to the end of the lake, and turned around. He gave that plane all the power it had. And he almost made it. At the last minute, the right wing tip hit a tree. The plane flipped, and they crashed. But they survived!

As they regained consciousness, one hunter moaned to the other, "Where are we?"

His companion painfully raised to one elbow and looked around. "About thirty yards farther than we were last year."

Little by little, athletes get further along the road to success as they work hard, practice, and try their best to do what, at the outset, may seem impossible.

Play As a Team

There is diversity within a sports team, yet it operates as one unit. One athlete pitches; another plays right field. One is quarterback; another is a defensive tackle. They aren't the same size. They don't make the same money. They don't get the same press coverage. But it takes all of them, playing their own positions to the best of their ability, to win games.

I was on the starting five in high-school basketball. We had a guy on the team who always shot the ball himself. He never passed it to anyone. When he got the ball, it was a foregone conclusion he was going to shoot. He scored a lot of points, but he also missed a lot of shots, and we lost a lot of games. The problem was that he didn't know anything about teamwork. It's important in sports and in the rest of life too. We have to know what our position is and play it as part of a team. That's the only way to win.

This lesson is very important in building a great church. We can't all be preachers or elders or Bible school teachers. Romans 12:5–8 is a great scripture that says we are one body but have different gifts. It lists seven of them: preaching, serving, teaching, encouraging, giving, leading, and showing mercy. Different people have different gifts; all are needed, working together, to form a healthy church.

First Corinthians 12:12–26 is laced with humor. It compares the church to a human body and has the different body parts talking to each other. The foot says, "Because I'm not a hand, I'm not part of the body."

How like us! We say, "If I were the preacher, I'd . . .," "I'll tell you what I'd do if I were an elder," "If I were a man," or "If I had money."

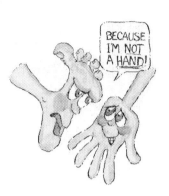

This little section of the New Testament tells us that God put all the parts in the body—the church—exactly as it pleased him, and each part, each one of us, is indispensable. Each of us has a part to do, a position to play.

Be Willing to Sacrifice Out

In baseball there is a play called the "sacrifice." A batter hits the ball strategically to force the opponents to field it in a way that takes him out of the game—either by catching a pop fly or throwing to first base. But while they're busy getting the batter out, the batter's teammate, already on base, advances. He may even score a run. Thus the batter makes a sacrifice for the good of the team.

The sacrifice reminds us that the primary concern is the team, whether it's a baseball squad or the church. In the same way, what we do as Christians affects the other people who comprise the church. Paul said: "I eagerly expect and hope that I will in no way be ashamed, but will have sufficient courage so that now as always Christ will be exalted in my body, whether by life or by death. For to me, to live is Christ and to die is gain" (Phil. 1:20–21).

When Christians put themselves as individuals second and concentrate on the good of the body first, great churches result. When church members recognize how others have sacrificed to benefit the whole church, a feeling of respect and camaraderie flows through the congregation.

Follow the Rules of the Game

Competitors in organized sports have rules to follow. There is an official rule book, and officials called "referees" or "umpires" enforce the rules and punish those who disobey them.

Jim Tunney, the great referee for the National Football League, was telling of a game he officiated for the Dallas Cowboys. When "Too Tall" Jones committed a foul, Tunney threw the flag, indicating a penalty was about to be imposed.

Jones had gotten his nickname because he was six-foot-eight and weighed almost three hundred pounds. Storming across the field, he towered over Tunney. Then he jerked the flag up off the turf—and *ate* it! It must have been quite a scene. But you know who won that argument, don't you?

I like to watch baseball when there is a close call at home plate. The umpire stabs his thumb into the air and shouts, "You're out!" The runner's manager comes storming off the bench, the teammates following in outraged protest. Manager and umpire are nose to nose, yelling so loudly they're red in the face, spitting all over each other. Caps get tossed in the air and thrown on the ground. Spiked shoes kick dust clouds six feet high. But when the dust clears, you know who wins!

There are rules in life too. And those who follow the rules do better than those who don't. We always have a choice. We can play by our own rules. We can dodge and twist and try to get by any way we want. But when the game is over, we'll find ourselves nose to nose with God. And you know who's going to win!

The Bible—our rule book—says we will be judged by the things written in the books, according to our works (see Rev. 20:12–13). Jesus said,

> Not everyone who says to me, "Lord, Lord," will enter the kingdom of heaven, but only he who does the will of my Father who is in heaven. Many will say to me on that day, "Lord, Lord, did we not prophesy in your name, and in your name drive out demons and perform many miracles?" Then I will tell them plainly, "I never knew you. Away from me, you evildoers!" (Matt. 7:21–23)

The Immortal Difference

In sports, only one team wins. And winning is everything to these teams. One year when Jim Tunney was to officiate at the Super Bowl he greeted John Madden, coach of the Oakland Raiders, by saying, "Congratulations, John, for being one of two teams out of twenty-eight to make it all the way to the Super Bowl!"

Well, just getting there wasn't enough for Madden. He shot back, "Congratulations to you, too, Jim. We took a vote on who was best of the ninety-two referees in the NFL. You came in second!"

Jim was impressed. Then his curiosity got the best of him. "John, who came in first?" he asked.

"It was a tie," quipped Madden, "between you and the other ninety-one!"

In life, our relationship with Jesus is everything. Nothing else—no one else—can tie with him for first place. When we play on his team, we are *all* winners. Not just in this game on earth but in eternity.

8

Rescue 911

In the book of Psalms, David portrays God as a loving father. Some people today get cheated out of having a good father, but we all instinctively know what one acts like, and God fits that role perfectly. Here's some of what Psalm 103:3–12 says about God:

- He forgives our sins.
- He heals our diseases.
- He has great love for his people.
- His blessings satisfy our deepest desires.
- He keeps us young.
- He will make things right for the oppressed.
- He is full of compassion and grace.
- He is slow to get angry and quick to get over it.

- He won't hold a grudge.
- He gives us what we need, not what we deserve!
- He flings our guilt to the winds!

What a God! But does this sound like church? Is this the way God's people act? Too many times the answer is no! We've been known to kill our wounded and freeze out those who are different from us, whether in race, education, or beliefs! Psalm 103 describes the character of God. It is what he wants his people to be like. It is what his church ought to be like!

The Thrill of the Rescue!

Rescue shows on TV are popular. *Rescue 911, ER, Chicago Hope,* and *M*A*S*H* all deal with finding people in crisis and saving them from danger. A typical show might follow this basic story-line: A little girl falls into a well and is stuck. The water is rising, and she'll soon be dead. But the men and women in uniform are on their way. They are professional, and they care. Emergency vehicles and equipment arrive. Within minutes, the child is brought to safety. Everyone cheers; it was all worth it. Afterward, we interview the heroes and heroines, and they say, "It was just my job." We eat it up!

Dial 911!

Everyone knows the number. We teach our kids to dial it in case of an emergency. When you need help in a hurry, it's your direct line to the police department, the fire department, and the hospital. They respond in minutes with flashing lights and screaming sirens.

And what does it cost? Some of it has been paid by our taxes and insurance, while some of it comes out of our pockets. But we don't

care about the cost when it's an emergency. We're just grateful someone is there—someone who cares, someone who is trained to rescue
us from tragedy.

Rescue in the Land Down Under

During a recent trip to Australia, I got a closer look at one of these
rescue operations. It was during the French Vendee Globe, a single-
man yacht race, which began on November 3. Sixteen contestants
entered, and the winner was to cross the finish line 105 days later.

Tony's Bullimore's yacht, the *Exide Challenger,* capsized in the
stormy seas on January 5. After spending four days in pitch black-
ness inside his overturned craft, Bullimore rigged a hammock just
above the water line and sent off distress signals. Australian rescue
planes picked up his frantic banging on the hull with their sonar and
radioed the HMAS *Adelaide* nearby.

The *Adelaide* raced to the scene and deployed a raft. The rescuers
pounded on the side of the overturned hull and cried out, "Are you
there?" Bullimore responded by diving into the icy waters and coming up at the raft. I was staying with friends just ten minutes away
from the scene, and we joined five thousand spectators to watch the
rescue attempt. It was exciting beyond belief; three governments
(France, England, and Australia) participated in it. It cost more than
ten million dollars, but everyone thought it was well worth the
money. We never stop to count the cost when lives are at stake.

Throwing Out the Spiritual Lifeline

Churches ought to feel this way about those in need of spiritual
rescue. All around us are people who have been blown away, people
who have been beat up and knocked down, people who are lost and

searching for the way back. God did more than spend millions on them; he gave his only Son. He knew that most of us would never appreciate his sacrifice and that many would not even acknowledge it, but he sent him anyway!

God wants us all to be rescued. Listen to the promise from Job 5:17–22:

> Do not despise the discipline of the Almighty. For he wounds, but he also binds up; he injures, but his hands also heal. From six calamities he will rescue you; in seven no harm will befall you. In famine he will ransom you from death, and in battle from the stroke of the sword. You will be protected from the lash of the tongue, and need not fear when destruction comes. You will laugh at destruction and famine, and need not fear the beasts of the earth.

Did he mention that some of those beasts walk on two legs? God's concern for us is echoed in the following verses:

> Who is like you O Lord? You rescue the poor from those too strong for them, the poor and needy from those who rob them. (Ps. 35:10)

> Even to your old age and gray hairs, I am he, I am he who will sustain you. I have made you and I will carry you; I will sustain you and I will rescue you. (Isa. 46:4)

> The Lord will rescue me from every evil attack and will bring me safely to his heavenly kingdom. To him be glory for ever and ever. Amen. (2 Tim. 4:18)

Spreading a Ministry of Reconciliation

As Christians, we must show this same concern to others. In 2 Corinthians 5:17–20, Paul writes,

> Therefore, if anyone is in Christ, he is a new creation; the old has gone, the new has come! All this is from God, who *reconciled* us to himself through Christ and gave us the ministry of *reconciliation*: that God was *reconciling* the world to himself in Christ, not counting men's sins against them. And he has committed to us the message of *reconciliation*. We are therefore Christ's ambassadors, as though God were making his appeal through us. We implore you on Christ's behalf: Be *reconciled* to God. (emphasis added)

This is what God is all about. It is the prime work of the church. To be reconciled means to be brought back together, to be restored, to be made whole again! God has entrusted us with the ministry of finding broken people and mending them, finding sick people and healing them. Our mission is to offer help, hope, solutions, and salvation to the world.

God has entrusted us with the ministry of finding broken people and mending them, finding sick people and healing them.

Oh, That Churches Would Wake Up!

One week when I was speaking in a Texas town, a man approached me hesitantly. He said, "You don't remember me, do you?" But I did! He was a preacher I lived close to years ago. He had blown it. He'd ruined his marriage, lost his ministry, and fallen away from the Lord. His body language said it all: "You don't want to have anything to do with me, do you?" I gave him a big hug and told him that I loved him—no matter what had happened in the past—and that God loved him, too, and wanted him back. He hadn't had too many people offer him such encouragement. Many dial 911, yet far too few receive an answer.

I spoke with a lovely lady recently who had become involved with another man. Two marriages had broken up as a result. They had tried to repent and return to the Lord. The man had even written a letter of apology to the church. He said I was the only one who had responded to it.

Sounds like a joke I once heard from comedian Hal Roach. "I called suicide prevention. They put me on hold!" he said. "I called 911, and they told me to go to hell!"

We laugh at the jokes, but it isn't funny when it happens to precious people for whom Jesus died.

I know of another preacher who fell. It had happened years ago, but the past caught up with him, and the scandal was exposed to the public. His church asked me to talk to them about what to do. Should they keep him and work for reconciliation? Or should they fire him and get rid of the problem? I'm so glad they opted for reconciliation! He's doing a great work for God today! I'm thankful that his church realized their work was one of reconciliation!

There's so much hurt out there. People mean well, but they fall into all kinds of pits. I wish we would surround them with love instead of pointed fingers, snarling lips, and angry voices.

James Robison, a television evangelist, told of a dream he once had. He saw an old man crying uncontrollably. "Old man," Robison said, "why are you crying?"

"Because of my children," the man said. "I have a little boy who is blind. His brothers and sisters tease him. They put things in front of him to make him fall. I have a teenage daughter who got pregnant out of wedlock. The kids have told everyone about her. They've made fun of her and called her names. I have an older boy who is in jail. They call him names. They won't write him or go see him. And they refuse to let him come home when he gets out of jail!"

"Who are you, old man?" Robison asked.

"I am Jesus," he replied, "and I'm talking about my church!"

Reverend Bill Hybels, senior pastor of the Willow Creek Community Church, took a survey in the Chicago area to find out why people did not go to church. The top three reasons were:

- They didn't like being bugged for money.
- They found church boring, predictable, and routine.
- They didn't think church was relevant to their lives.

How did we get so far off track? We talk of buildings, buses, and budgets. We concern ourselves with carpet, cooling, and committees. In our efforts to become dignified, we've become downright petrified. Jesus died for *people!* And the deeper in sin you are, the more you fit into that category.

A Clear Vision of the Church

What did Jesus have in mind when he said, "On this rock I will build my church"? (Matt. 16:18). If you want to understand his vision for the church, read about Simon the Pharisee and the prostitute (see Luke 7:36–50). Simon gave a dinner party for Jesus. He wanted to impress this VIP with his elegance. A prostitute crashed the party and poured her heart out at Jesus' feet. To Simon, she ruined the party. To Jesus, she made the party. Her tears fell on Jesus' feet, and she wiped them with her hair. Jesus gave his marvelous grace and salvation to that fallen woman. Many churches today see the stained glass but miss the stained person. In this story, Jesus rebukes Simon, and us, for failing to see what counts.

Do you want to know what the church is supposed to be like? Read about the prodigal son (see Luke 15:11–24). We can empathize with him because we've all wandered far away from God. The boy sinned before God and shamed the family name. But then he woke up and decided to come home. Thank God it wasn't to a cold, sophisticated church. In verse 20, Jesus says, "But while he was still a long way off, his father saw him and was filled with compassion for him; he ran to his son, threw his arms around him and kissed him."

That's church! If that isn't happening where you worship, hurry and repair your Rescue 911 line.

The church is a hospital, not a prison. It is a place of reconciliation, not a country club for the elite. Most of all, it is a family made up of all kinds, not an exclusive aristocracy of the rich and famous.

Hello? 911? Is anyone there?

9

Learn to Brake before You Break

Marge Baker, a friend of our family for more than fifty years, has really been through the pits lately. She recently wrote me an upbeat letter, sharing what she's been going through during the past few years. She was exposed to toxic materials. Her body is producing a protein that destroys her DNA cells. Arthritis has affected her head, neck, and optic nerves. She lost one kidney to cancer. She's been hearing words like "no cure."

Yet she knows God is still in control. Her letter was written to cheer me up and keep me motivated after my retirement as senior minister of a Tulsa church. I called her, and we mutually cheered each other up. She mentioned wanting to write a book with a chapter titled, "Learn to Brake before You Break." I asked permission to do it as a session on my TV show, *Peak of the Week Live!,* and to include it as a chapter in this book. Marge, thank you so much!

Stress Is a Universal Condition

Stress is the leading cause of heart attacks, high blood pressure, hypertension, colitis, migraines, ulcers, diabetes, allergies, and indigestion. It leads to depression, mental breakdowns, and even suicide! The word *stress* comes from the Latin word *strictus,* meaning "uptight."

Not all stress is bad. In fact, stress is the normal condition of winning. The 100-meter dash is a good example. The starter gives three commands. First, he says, "On your mark!" All the athletes get "loosey goosey," trying to totally relax their minds and bodies. Then he says, "Get set," and you've never seen such tension. All outside sounds are shut out. Every muscle in the body is strained and prepared to break into action. Then at the word "Go!" they push off with all their might. And the one who manages stress best crosses the finish line first!

Out-of-
control
stress
leads to
distress.

But out-of-control stress leads to *distress.* The late Dr. Norman Vincent Peale told of meeting with one of his parishioners. The man's head was down, and he was mumbling out loud, blasting his problems. "These [blankety-blank] problems," he said. Dr. Peale said he was using some spiritual terms, but not in a spiritual manner. Dr. Peale confronted his friend. "George, what seems to be the problem?" "Oh, hello, Dr. Peale," George said. "It's just these problems. They're driving me crazy. I can't get anywhere. If I could just get rid of my problems, then I could really get things done!" To which Dr. Peale replied, "You know, George, I was just speaking in upstate New York. There were thirty thousand people there who had no problems at all!" George was excited, "Show me to the place. That's the spot for me!" he said. In Dr. Peale's inimitable way, he said, "Well, I was at Forrest Lawn Cemetery! None of those people have any problems!"

Dead people don't have problems; only people who are facing life and getting things done have problems. Problems constitute a sign of life. The more problems you have, the more alive you are. Could I see the hands of those of you who are really living?

Take a Break from Stress

It's normal to have stress, but we've got to have relief every now and then. We'll get it one way or another. We'll either learn to brake before we break, or we'll have a nervous breakdown, if we don't become suicidal! Someone once said, "It isn't what happens to you, but what you *do* about what happens to you!" Here are several ways to handle stress.

Laugh Yourself Healthy

I once heard of a northeast university that had a "scream break" every afternoon at two o'clock. They loved to surprise visitors on campus who were unaware of this activity. Students would be sitting under a tree talking, walking to and from the cafeteria or the library, or studying in their dorm rooms as usual. But when the clock struck two, the entire campus would stand up and scream for two minutes at the top of their lungs. It's not a bad idea. How about having a scream break at your home or office every day?

When I scream for two minutes, I'm exhausted, but when I laugh for a few minutes, I'm refreshed and energized. I even have new creativity. Laughter gives you real relief from stress. That's why I recommend that you cultivate a good sense of humor. Watch funny movies! Why anyone wants to watch misery and trauma on TV and in movies is beyond me. I'm a *Pink Panther* fan, and I have all six movies of that series. Come over and we'll watch them together. I'll guarantee it's a good stress reliever.

Make Time for Five-Minute Vacations

I listened once to a tape called *Take Five-Minute Vacations!* Terrific! We've all been somewhere, sometime when we were really at peace with the world and ourselves. Close your eyes and remember. You can recall every little detail—colors, smells, and feelings. See, you can escape to there anytime you want. Here's one of mine.

I've made several trips to the Bible lands. I especially like to visit the Garden of Gethsemane. The Bible says Jesus went there often to pray with his disciples. I've been there with a group at 4:00 A.M. The sun rises over Bethany, and rays shine on the dome of the mosque close to where the temple once stood. Olive trees are there that might have been there when Jesus prayed in the garden. We find ourselves a tree to sit under, and the meditation is incredible! Someone always starts that beautiful song by C. Austin Miles.

> I come to the garden alone,
> While the dew is still on the roses;
> And the voice I hear,
> Falling on my ear,
> The Son of God discloses.
>
> He speaks, and the sound of His voice
> Is so sweet the birds hush their singing;

And the melody that He gave to me,
Within my heart is ringing.
And He walks with me,
And He talks with me,
And He tells me I am His own;
And the joy we share
As we tarry there,
None other has ever known.

You have places like this too. Perhaps it's a babbling brook or a special vacation spot—places full of beautiful memories to recall and relive. Retreat there as often as you like. It's a marvelous stress reliever and soul reviver!

Find a Balance between Work and Rest

Oh, the Bible talks about work. Man was put in the garden to work it (see Gen. 2:15). Jesus charged the disciples to "go and work today in the vineyard" (Matt. 21:28). He also said, "We must do the work of him who sent me" (John 9:4).

But the Bible also talks about rest. God rested on the seventh day of creation (see Gen. 2:2). Why did he rest? Was he tired? No, I think it was to exemplify how we should live. David said, "My soul finds rest in God alone" (Ps. 62:1), and "He who dwells in the shelter of the Most High will rest in the shadow of the Almighty" (Ps. 91:1). Even Jesus urged, "Come to me, all you who are weary and burdened, and I will give you rest. Take my yoke upon you and learn from me, for I am gentle and humble in heart, and you will find rest for your souls. For my yoke is easy and my burden is light" (Matt. 11:28–30).

And here's another classic: "And he saith unto them, Come . . . apart into a desert place, and rest a while. For there were many coming and going, and they had no leisure so much as to eat." (Mark 6:31 ASV).

Wow! Like someone said, "If you don't 'come apart' . . . you *will!*"

Develop a Relationship with the One Who Brings Peace

Not only does Jesus offer forgiveness and purpose, but he also

brings peace. In fact, the three are interwoven and inseparable! As David said, "Even though I walk through the valley of the shadow of death, I will fear no evil, for you are with me" (Ps. 23:4).

There's a funny story about L. O. Sanderson's song, "Be with Me, Lord." Many couples have used it in their weddings over the years. Sanderson told of one couple who wanted him to marry them, but they wanted to use another song they had become fond of, "Dear Lord and Father of Mankind" by John G. Whittier. Sanderson advised, "Maybe you ought to listen to the words before you have it sung at your wedding!" It goes like this,

> Dear Lord and Father of mankind,
> Forgive our foolish ways;
> Reclothe us in our rightful mind . . .

The couple chose to go with "Be with Me, Lord."

Yet, "Dear Lord and Father of Mankind" has a marvelous verse about "braking."

> Drop thy still dews of quietness,
> Till all our strivings cease;

Learn to Brake before You Break

Take from our souls the strain and stress,
And let our ordered lives confess
The beauty of thy peace.

I once heard Richard Rogers, a preacher from Lubbock, Texas, say, "When I wake up in the morning, I reach for my Bible. I check to see if Romans 8:28 is still there. If it is, I get up and go about business as usual. If ever it's not, I'll just go back to bed." That verse reads, "And we know that in all things God works for the good of those who love him, who have been called according to his purpose."

So learn to apply the brakes before you break! You'll live longer, and you'll be so much nicer to be around!

10

How to Become a Classic instead of an Old Wreck

For more than sixty years, Paul Wright has been helping adult drivers sharpen their skills and refresh their knowledge of driving laws. Although he's ninety-three years old, he shows no signs of quitting anytime soon.

He was born in Enid, Oklahoma, in 1904, during the "horse and buggy days"—literally! He's seen a lot of changes in cars and highways during his life. He remembers when the speed limit was thirty miles per hour and the roads were paved only to the edge of town. He has a great sense of humor too. One of his favorite lines to use in class is "What is a nanosecond?" After a pause, he adds the punch line with a twinkle in his eye, "The time between when the light turns green and the guy behind you honks his horn!"

Most of Paul's students are over fifty years old. He's a good example to them, and to us, that we have a choice. We can become a classic . . . instead of an old wreck!

How Do You Know When You're Getting Old?

There are a lot of cute sayings out there to show us when we're getting old. You know you're getting old when . . .

- Everything hurts. And what doesn't hurt, doesn't work!
- The gleam in your eye is from the sun hitting your bifocals!
- You feel like the night before and you haven't been anywhere!
- Your little black book only contains names that end with M.D!
- You get winded playing cards!
- You know all the answers, but nobody asks you the questions! (Or, you know all the answers, but they've changed the questions!)
- You look forward to a dull evening!
- You need glasses . . . to find your glasses!
- You sit in a rocking chair, but you can't get it going!
- Your knees buckle, but your belt won't!
- Your back goes out more than you do!
- You've got too much room in the house and not enough room in your medicine cabinet!
- You sink your teeth into a steak . . . and they stay there!

Here's a good question: Did you ever feel like you were living in the fast lane but were married to a speed bump? Maybe you've heard the old saying, It's tragic to face your golden years without any gold!

When I turned sixty-five, I got an AARP card, a Medicare card, and senior discount cards by the dozen. I can deal them like poker—pick a card, any card! I went to the movies in Australia, and they let me in on pensioner rates.

I remember when I was fifty-eight. We were having breakfast with a few friends. It occurred to me that Denny's gives senior discounts early, so I asked the cashier, "At what age do you give senior discounts?" "I don't know; I'll ask!" she said. Then she yelled at the top of her voice, "Larry, at what age do we give senior discounts?" A million eyes peered at me. Larry stuck his head out of the kitchen and looked me over. "Give it to him!" he said. Since then, I've always made a point to leave my chewing gum in the hot sauce when I eat at Denny's!

Secrets to Living Longer

More Americans are "graying" these days, and many of them fear getting old. They equate it with senility and poverty or with becoming useless and hopeless! More than thirty-six thousand people in America are over one hundred years old. Many of these people are active, healthy, alert, and contributing.

20/20 did a study of ninety-six independent, noninstitutionalized people over one hundred. It was amazing! You'd think the common thread among them would be a healthy diet, regular exercise, or good genes. Instead, they found that they had four qualities in common.

1. Optimism

Geneva McDaniel, 106, attributed her longevity to optimism. "Think positive! Don't get negative," she said. "Don't think about yourself. Just go out and do what you have to do!" Jesse Champion, 106, quipped, "The Lord let me live to see all those who treated me bad die!" Champion, and his wife, Phronie, 85, go to church twice a week and believe a deep religious faith is the most important thing in life. These people are "unbuggable." They're not easily upset. It just goes to show that attitude is everything! I keep promising one of these days to do a weekly TV program called *Crotchety Is a Choice!* Because, of course, it is!

2. Commitment to a Project or a Cause

People need involvement outside themselves. Whether it's hobbies, education, or religion, we all need something to devote ourselves to. I was talking to one lady about her involvement in church. I asked her, "What do you have a passion for?" Her eyes lit up. "Do you know how to spell *passion?*" she asked. *"Pass-I-on!"* It's what we pour ourselves into that counts, which is another good reason to be active in your local church.

3. Mobility

Exercise is so important! Almost all those interviewed participated in some form of exercise! Geneva McDaniel teaches aerobics at her senior center, and of course, her positive attitude plays an important role there too!

4. Ability to Cope with Loss

The longer you live, the more you lose. We all lose things eventually—our health, job, car, and house. And the list goes on and on!

Before long, we lose people—parents, spouses, brothers, sisters, friends, relatives, and children. That is, if you don't go first! One lady laughed that she had lived so long that those who had gone on before her must think she didn't make it! One reason the elderly fear death less is because they have so many loved ones waiting for them on the other shore.

The Pleasures of Age

You Get to See How It All Turns Out

You get to see if nice guys really do finish last, and you get to witness your own life unfold (drama or comedy, as the case may be). You see the Dow Jones averages rise and fall and rise again! You get to see changes; life is full of changes. They can be thrilling or terrifying! It's your choice! Cars change. They don't make cars like they used to. Aren't we glad? Clothes change. Fashion is fickle. Home appliances and luxuries change and get cheaper! TV stars come and go. A politician can have his face on *Time* one week and be *doing time* the next!

Over the years, we watch attacks on the Bible, the church, morality, and Jesus Christ. As time passes, biblical values stand firm. You'll find that over the long haul, people regret acting immorally, marrying too flippantly, quitting too soon, or leaving the church. People never regret, however, living a life committed to Jesus Christ! By the time the fat lady sings, you've seen quite a show and should be able to grin your way through eternity!

By the time the fat lady sings, you've seen quite a show and should be able to grin your way through eternity!

CHAPTER TEN

You Get to Stop Doing the Things You Don't Enjoy

Duty will always be there, and no one ever regrets responding to it. But as you get older, you stop doing things for the sake of appearance. I never liked wearing a tie. When you think about it, it's a sadistic piece of material. It blocks your vocal chords and squeezes your windpipe so you can't breathe—what a thing for a preacher to wear. When I get to heaven, I'm gonna look up the guy who invented the tie and give him a piece of my mind. Come to think of it, maybe he won't be there!

I retired from the pulpit in June 1996. Now I get to do all the things I enjoy. I preach more than ever. I've traveled to Australia, South Africa, and literally coast to coast encouraging God's people. I have time to sit with the elderly, laugh at their stories, weep over their pain, and pray for their faith. The time deadlines are gone. I don't go to business meetings or serve on any committees that I don't choose to serve on. I leave the politics and the mundane to others. I'll pray for them, of course, with a smile on my face!

You Finally Learn You Don't Have to Win All the Arguments

I still have passionate opinions, but I don't argue with people who aren't smart enough to know I'm right! They bellow their facts while I just smile and say, "Hmmmmm." It drives them nuts and saves my breath. I've learned my list of necessities is very short. I don't waste my time arguing about things that aren't essential to salvation. I'm going to work on getting people to commit to Christ, respect his Word, worship in his church, and live lives worth sharing with others. That's what really counts!

You Finally Start Choosing Comfort over Style

It's the tie thing again. I'm finding out that people aren't nearly as impressed with my expensive suits as I once thought. I'm like the woman in the shoe store who said, "Well, I wear a size seven. But these eights feel so good, I believe I'll take a nine!"

You Start Getting More Help Than Ever Before

I pass through a lot of airports nowadays. If I slump my shoulders a bit and walk with a slight limp, they'll put me on one of those little carts, take me to my gate, and board me first.

I'm not expected to remember things anymore either. If someone says, "You don't remember me, do you?" I say, "Of course not, I'm over sixty-five!" If they say, "Do you remember me?" I say, "Sure. When did you get out?" People don't ask me to help move heavy things anymore. I just tell them where to put it!

You Begin to Know What Love Is All About

By the time you get old, you've made all the mistakes in the book and maybe a few not in the books yet. You become more tolerant of those who stumble and make mistakes. You find out that a true friend is one who knows all about you and loves you anyway—kind of like Jesus does! You also should have learned the secret of the universe by now.

It's written in Luke 6:38: "Give, and it will be given you. A good measure, pressed down, shaken together and running over. . . . For with the measure you use, it will be measured to you."

The great secret is getting by giving! So become a giver!

CHAPTER TEN

You Have Time to Smell the Roses

They've always been there, and they've always been sweet. But youth and pressures kept you from noticing. You've been there—fought the battles, bitten the bullets, and learned the lessons. It's someone else's turn to fight the dragons. Let them get lathered up in the arena. It's your turn to smell the roses.

You Find You're Still in the Driver's Seat of Life

You can champion any cause, make time for any ministry, or take your life in any direction you choose. You always have a choice. Susan Strasberg, a lady who was interviewed for the *20/20* survey, said, "I feel like a good bottle of wine. The older I get, the better I become. By the time I'm ninety, I'll be just about ready to uncork!"

Right on, Susan. Let the party begin!

11

Learn to Succeed by Failing

You've seen that Michael Jordan commercial: "I've missed nine thousand shots. I've lost three hundred games. Twenty-six times, I've been entrusted to take the game-winning shot—and missed! I've failed over and over again in my life. And that's why I succeed!"

Galatians 6:9 says the same thing in a nutshell. "Let us not become weary in doing good, for at the proper time we will reap a harvest if we do not give up."

Facing the Fear of Failure

Six hundred psychology majors were asked about their greatest fear. Their answer was "that I just don't have what it takes." Can you believe it? But they do! And you do too! Michael Jordan says it so eloquently in the commercial. The secret to success is not in talent, beauty, brains, or who your parents are. Success is 2 percent inspiration and 98 percent perspiration! It's hanging in there, baby. It's keeping on keeping on!

Find something you're really good at. Are you good at sailing, painting (houses or pictures), writing, teaching, fishing, or speaking?

How many are good at failing? Oh, I see bunches of hands up! Good! It's a very good quality to have. You can really use it to succeed.

What do you want to be good at? Making money? Playing sports? Building a career or business? How about making friends or forming good, long-lasting relationships like marriage? How about building a good character, name, and reputation? How about becoming an effective, committed Christian or doing some great project for God?

Great! Then do it the Michael Jordan way. Fail a lot while sincerely trying. Just keep at it. You'll come out on top if you don't quit!

Practicing for Success

Anything worth doing is worth doing poorly. That's right, poorly!

No one does it great the first time. We have to fail some in our attempts to get it right.

Babe Ruth set the strikeout record on his way to becoming the home run king. Abraham Lincoln ran for several different offices and failed miserably many times. But he kept on! He went on to become one of the most well-known and beloved presidents of the United States.

There once was a boy named Tommy who had dreamed of playing professional football since he was ten years old. He worked at it all through high school and college, and eventually the New Orleans

Learn to Succeed by Failing

Saints signed him as a place kicker. The game that brought him fame was one against the Detroit Lions. Time was running out in the fourth quarter; the Lions were leading seventeen to sixteen. The Saints had the ball with less than two minutes to go. Billy Kilmer passed to their forty-yard line. Time-out was called with two seconds left on the clock. Tom Dempsey came in to try for the game-winning field goal. The ball was snapped. The kick was in the air when the gun sounded the end of the game, and it was good! Tom Dempsey won the game for the Saints. He also kicked a sixty-three-yard field goal—setting a new record in professional football.

The remarkable thing about Tom Dempsey is that he has only one normal hand and no toes on his kicking foot! However, that's not even the amazing part! Let's go back to when little Tommy was ten years old and tried his first kick. The other kids were merciless. They laughed at him and said, "Look at Tommy. He thinks he's going to kick that ball. He'll land right on his backside!" And he did! But he wouldn't quit. He kept kicking footballs until one of them went through the goalpost, then another and another. Finally, most of them were going through from every angle and from incredible distances.

Imagine that record-setting kick. Imagine the pressure with fifty thousand fans screaming at the top of their lungs. Someone asked Tom Dempsey later, "How does a handicapped guy kick a ball like that?" Quickly, Tom replied, "I don't look at myself as handicapped. You can't worry about what you don't have. You've got to take what you *do* have and use it to your greatest potential. That's called blooming where you are

You can't worry about what you don't have. You've got to take what you do have and use it to your greatest potential.

planted!" Tom Dempsey did it the Michael Jordan way. He succeeded through failing!

Successful Failures in the Bible

Abraham

Abraham was seventy-five years old and childless, yet God called him to go to a land that he would show him. Abraham went fearlessly, but he failed several times on the way. Since Sarah, his wife, was such a beautiful woman, he always feared that someone might kill him to get her or that she would be taken from him during their travels. He told Sarah to tell everyone she was his sister. Talk about cowardice. Later, after waiting years for a son, Sarah tried to help God out by giving Abraham her handmaid to have a child by. This displeased God, yet Abraham corrected his mistakes. He kept hanging in there. In Hebrews 11, Abraham got the longest mention in Faith's Hall of Fame (vv. 8–19). He failed a lot, but he hung in there to win!

Moses

Surely we see Moses as a winner, but he wasn't always one. He tried to chicken out on God's call to leadership using the following list of excuses (see Exod. 3:13; 4:1, 10):

- "Nobody will listen to me!"
- "They'll ask, 'Who sent you?' and what will I say?"
- "What if they don't believe me?"
- "I can't talk well!"

Because of another failure, God would not let Moses enter the

Promised Land with the rest of Israel. But we remember him best as the man who led Israel from Egyptian bondage, rallied the Israelites at the Red Sea, and gave the Ten Commandments.

Someone who watched the movie *The Ten Commandments* said, "Moses is the guy who made Charlton Heston famous!"

Moses has his own space in Faith's Hall of Fame (see Heb. 11:23–29). Although he failed many times, he just kept on keeping on. So must you and I!

David

Just look at the way the script of David's life reads (see 1 Sam. 13:14; Acts 13:22).

> Scene 1: David kills Goliath.
> Scene 2: God makes David king.
> Scene 3: David commits adultery with Bathsheba.
> Scene 4: David is brought to accountability by Nathan.
> Scene 5: David repents and gets back on track.
> Scene 6: David is called a man after God's own heart!

David made some serious blunders, but he refused to throw up his hands and quit. He repented and moved on, each time becoming more devoted to God than before.

Simon Peter

Simon Peter is a classic example of a successful failure. He was chosen as an apostle of Jesus and was the first to name Jesus as the Christ (see Matt. 16:16). When Jesus foretold that his disciples would forsake him at the cross, Peter rebuked his Lord. "Even if all fall away, I will not" (Mark 14:29). And he meant it. But he did fall, in the worst way.

Judas came with the mob, and the other disciples ran away. Peter followed at a distance for a while, but then came the real fall. During Jesus' trial before the high priest, Peter was recognized in the nearby courtyard. He was accused of being one of Jesus' disciples. He denied it, three times. When Peter heard the rooster crow and realized what he had done, the Scriptures say, "The Lord turned and looked straight at Peter" (Luke 22:61). Then Peter went out and wept bitterly.

He's down! He's outta there! Peter, the man who so fiercely promised his loyalty couldn't even stand up against a little pressure.

But Jesus wasn't through with him yet. He picked this "failure" to preach the first Gospel sermon in Jerusalem (see Acts 2). He was also the first one to take the Gospel to the Gentiles (see Acts 10). He even wrote two books in the New Testament. Yet, he made so many mistakes. Can you relate? But he wouldn't quit.

You and Me

I find it hard to relate to Bible heroes. They seem too up there, too high and mighty. It helps to know they were humans just like you and me. The Bible says that the prophet Elijah was a man just like us (see James 5:17). Those who accomplished so much were men and women who often failed. The key was not in their mistakes but in what they did about them.

What have you failed at and need to try again? What are your unfulfilled dreams? Failures are things, not people! And as the old saying goes: One mistake doth not a failure make!

Well, did it work for Michael Jordan? Recently I watched game one of the NBA playoffs. The man who had missed nine thousand shots, lost three hundred games, and missed the game-winning shot twenty-six times, was again entrusted with the ball. Swish! The man who had failed so often came through as a winner once again!

You're getting the point, aren't you?

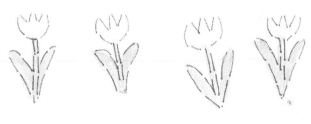

12

Random Acts of Kindness; Senseless Deeds of Beauty

I was getting out of my truck at a shopping center, and a lady pulled in ahead of me who had a bumper sticker that read "Practice Random Acts of Kindness; Senseless Deeds of Beauty!" I liked it. It motivated me. That lady will never know she missed out on twenty dollars. I had planned to walk by, hand her a twenty-dollar bill, and say, "Nice bumper sticker," then disappear into the mall. But she was gone before I got to her car. No matter, I'll pass it along to someone else. It just reminded me to keep an eye open for opportunities to do kind and beautiful things at every chance!

There are lots of other good ones around. I used to have one on my pickup truck that said "Have You Hugged Your Kid Today?" One day I pulled up at a bowling alley, and as I started for the door, a young boy about twelve came up to me and said, "Well, have you?" "Have I what?" I said. "Hugged your kid today!" he said. "No, she's in college about a hundred miles away. But thanks for reminding me. I'll do it as soon as I can!" I said.

Practicing Kindness from a Tollbooth

I read "Dear Ann" and "Dear Abby" every day. One letter was titled "Essay Inspires Random Acts of Kindness." Someone was still pushing that bumper sticker with its marvelous philosophy of life. A lady from Carbondale, Illinois wrote, "Ann, I've learned so much from you. Today I want to pass on what I've learned to others!" She sent in a little piece called "Conspiracy to Kindness!" It talked about a woman who told the attendant at a highway tollbooth that she wanted to pay the toll for the next six cars. Imagine the surprise on those people's faces as the toll attendant told each one, "Your toll has been paid by someone ahead of you!"

The lady who paid the toll had seen the message "Practice Random Acts of Kindness; Senseless Deeds of Beauty!" taped to a friend's refrigerator. Her friend had seen it on a warehouse wall and copied it on the back of an envelope and attached it to her fridge. She said she thought it was a message from God! Her husband, a teacher, took it to his school and posted it on the bulletin board for all his students to see. And the "toll payer" asked her local newspaper to print it.

So the message is spreading. It shows up on bumper stickers, business cards, and in the most unlikely places. It's catchy and intriguing! As it spreads, its mission is accomplished. A young man was motivated to clear his elderly neighbor's driveway. A teenage boy decided to mow his neighbor's yard. It reminds me of my next-door neighbor who mows across our property line by about twenty feet so he can reach my driveway and mow around the eight redbud trees spaced there. Someone else planted daffodils in an out-of-the-way place for others to enjoy. People are out there looking for countless ways to practice random acts of kindness and senseless deeds of beauty!

Look at the positive effect it has on its participants. They feel as if their burdens are lifted. They walk with a spring in their step. Their faces are full of joy. They feel motivated to "pass it on" to others!

Building a Better World

Many years ago, I ran across a tract titled, *A Better World Begins with Me!* It was written by Becky Burris and distributed by the R. W. Fair Foundation in Tyler, Texas.

Becky noticed that newspapers constantly screamed about hurts in the world—crime, violence, and man's inhumanity to man. She thought, *I can't just sit here twiddling my thumbs. That won't make anything better.* More guns, more bombs, and larger armies have not solved our problems either. As a popular song says, "What the world needs now is love, sweet love!" We've got to fill this world with love. Becky pointed out that love is free. "It lies all around us, waiting to be picked up, nourished, and shared!" she said.

But where do I start? she thought. *Someone has to start. Why not me? I have to begin somewhere, so why not here?* She started reading Bible passages about love. Then she began a mental and spiritual housecleaning. "You can't teach what you don't know, and you can't lead where you won't

Love is free. "It lies all around us, waiting to be picked up, nourished, and shared!"

go!" she said. She asked God to help her clear out all selfishness, whining, and faultfinding. She begged God to fill her and her world with thoughts and deeds of love! She started with her husband and young son, telling them often that she loved them. She did lots of hugging and poured on words of encouragement.

Then she branched out into the neighborhood where an eighty-

four-year-old lady lived next-door. Becky had always planned to go over there someday and visit. They had a delightful talk filled with hugs, kisses, laughter, and tears. She was so glad she went, because in the next few weeks, the lady slipped into a coma and died with a smile on her face.

Becky recruited and developed a group of people like herself. They call themselves "Better Worlders!" One said, "I put cookies out for the garbage man!" Another said, "I call people on the phone just to tell them I like them!" The golden rule is their motto. It says, "Do to others as you would have them do to you" (Luke 6:31).

Love Makes Up the Core of Scripture

Scripture contains a lot of messages about how to love others. Paul addresses the subject of unconditional love in Romans 12:19–21:

> Love from the center of who you are; don't fake it. Run for dear life from evil; hold on for dear life to good. . . . Practice playing second fiddle.

Keep yourself fueled and aflame. Be alert servants . . . cheerfully expectant. Don't quit in hard times; pray all the harder. Help needy Christians; be inventive in hospitality.

Bless your enemies. . . . Laugh with your happy friends; . . . share tears when they're down. Get along with each other; don't be stuck-up. Make friends with nobodies; don't be the great somebody.

Don't hit back; discover beauty in everyone. . . . Don't insist on getting even.

Buy [your enemy] lunch. . . . Your generosity will surprise him with goodness. Get the best of evil by doing good. (*MSG*)

And in Luke 6:30–38, Jesus says:

Live generously. . . .

Give without expecting a return. . . .

Don't pick on people, jump on their failures, criticize their faults. . . . Be easy on people; you'll find life a lot easier. Give away your life; you'll find life given back . . . with bonus and blessing. Giving, not getting, is the way. Generosity begets generosity. (*MSG*)

Ephesians 4:32 expresses the same thought. "Be gentle with one another, sensitive. Forgive one another as quickly and thoroughly as God in Christ forgave you" (*MSG*).

First Corinthians 13:4–8 also has a marvelous definition of love.

This love of which I speak is slow to lose patience—it looks for a way of being constructive. It is not possessive: it is neither anxious to impress nor does it cherish inflated ideas of its own importance.

CHAPTER TWELVE

Love has good manners and does not pursue selfish advantage. It is not touchy. It does not keep account of evil or gloat over the wickedness of other people. On the contrary, it is glad with all good men when truth prevails.

Love knows no limit to its endurance, no end to its trust, no fading of its hope; it can outlast anything. It is, in fact, the one thing that still stands when all else has fallen. (PHILLIPS)

The little Vacation Bible School song says it so well:

Love is something, if you give it away,
Give it away; give it away.
Love is something, if you give it away,
You'll end up having more!

Love is like a shiny penny,
Hold it tight, and you won't have any.
Give it away, and you'll have plenty.
You'll end up having more!

I watched a young man looking at Valentine cards in the store. His body language told a sad story. He found a card he really liked. He looked at the price, but the expression on his face told me he didn't have enough money. He began to look at other less expensive ones. I pulled out five dollars and handed it to him. "Go for it," I said. He protested, but I hurried out of the store. It felt really good!

One of the things I'm enjoying most about my retirement is visiting with the elderly, the sick, and the shut-ins. I've known most of these people for a couple of decades. They appreciate it so much and tell me so. But, my, how rewarding it is for me. I just sit and listen. I dote on them and tell them how they're loved and appreciated. I don't know anything that takes so little time and energy and reaps more dividends.

Just a Few Suggestions

Some of you are going to be really motivated by that bumper sticker! Here are a few suggestions. Then come up with some of your own! Go for it!

- Be courteous in traffic; let people in!
- Speak random words of encouragement like, "I know something good about you!"
- Send newspaper clippings of others to them with a note saying, "I'm proud of you!"
- Phone a friend you haven't spoken to in years.
- Say "I love you" lots of times and to lots of people.
- Say "I'm sorry" even when it isn't your fault!
- Give lots of hugs!
- Smile a lot at everybody! Someone once said, "Smiling won't solve everything, but it will make folks wonder what you've been up to!
- Share the love of Jesus with someone who doesn't know him!

Acts of kindness and beauty begin slowly and with a single word or deed, but they can end in an avalanche that will beautify and enrich the whole earth.

What a marvelous epidemic you and I can start. Soon millions will be doing random acts of kindness and senseless deeds of beauty. Get going!

Get Out of the Kitchen

In an earlier chapter, I referred to G. E. and Girt McElheny. Since I began writing this book, they have both passed away. They were dear friends who died within six weeks of each other. This chapter, like "Eye in the Sky," came from ideas G. E. gave me. I write this one in their memory!

As they continued their travel, Jesus entered a village. A woman by the name of Martha welcomed him and made him feel quite at home. She had a sister, Mary, who sat before the Master, hanging on every word he said. But Martha was pulled away by all she had to do in the kitchen. Later, she stepped in, interrupting them. "Master, don't you care that my sister has abandoned the kitchen to me? Tell her to lend me a hand."

CHAPTER THIRTEEN

The Master said, "Martha, dear Martha, you're fussing far too much and getting yourself worked up over nothing. One thing only is essential, and Mary has chosen it—it's the main course, and won't be taken from her." (Luke 10:38–42 MSG)

Bethany was only a stone's throw from Jerusalem. In fact, you can see it from the Mount of Olives. Jesus often went there, or rather escaped there, to be with Mary, Martha, and Lazarus. The Bible says, "Jesus loved Martha and her sister and Lazarus" (John 11:5). Tonight, Jesus was a guest in their home.

The Dinner Party

There's Jesus, relaxing after a long, hard day of teaching and preaching in the marketplace and synagogue. Martha is in the kitchen preparing another one of her delicious dinners.

John 12:2 says that "Lazarus was among those reclining at the table with [Jesus]," indicating there were others there for this meal.

Then there's Mary, sitting at the feet of Jesus. She's got that look on her face again. She loves Jesus and probably suspects he is the promised Messiah. Her eyes shine with radiance as she hangs on to his every word. Martha notices Mary's inactivity every time she comes into the room to refill their glasses and to inquire if they need anything else.

Finally, it gets the best of this most congenial of women.

Martha has had all she can stand. "They're in there having fun while I'm in here doing all the work," she mutters under her breath.

Wringing her apron around her hands, she says in a loud voice, "Can I get a little help in here please? Jesus, tell Mary to get in the kitchen and help me get this food on the table!"

Why was she so upset? Was it because she was doing all the work and getting no help? Or was she wishing that she, too, could be part of the sweet fellowship going on in the living room? Jesus' reply is enlightening. "Martha, dear Martha. You're fussing far too much. You're getting worked up over nothing. Only one thing is essential. Mary has chosen it! And it won't be taken from her" (see Luke 10:41–42).

Martha, Charming Servant and Hostess!

Martha is mentioned thirteen times in Scripture, and each time the text describes how she welcomed Jesus and made him feel at home. In John 11 and 12, she welcomes Jesus to her home after her brother, Lazarus, has died. That time she chided Jesus for not coming sooner. After all, he could have prevented her brother from dying.

The Bible always pictures Martha as serving! You think, *Good old Martha. We need a lot more women like her!* Her words and actions speak for themselves:

- Martha opened her home to Jesus. (Luke 10:38)
- "Martha was distracted by all the preparations that had to be made." (Luke 10:40)
- Martha was worried and upset about many things. (Luke 10:41,
- Martha went out to meet Jesus, but Mary stayed at home. (John 11:20)
- "Lord, if you had been here, my brother would not have died." (John 11:21)

- Martha served while Lazarus reclined at the table with Jesus. (John 12:2)

The Kitchen Is a Good Place to Be!

Duty and responsibility are noble things. There are too few who are busy, active, obedient, committed, and involved, and too many who are lazy, apathetic, and selfish. Some ride on the coattails of other people's faith. In fact, the chief critics in the church are usually those who watch but do not do!

Jesus had a high regard for duty:

> As long as it is day, we must do the work of him who sent me. Night is coming, when no one can work. (John 9:4)

> Although he was a son, he learned obedience from what he suffered and, once made perfect, he became the source of eternal salvation for all who obey him. (Heb. 5:8–9)

> Blessed are they that do his commandments, that they may have right to the tree of life, and may enter in through the gates into the city. (Rev. 22:14 KJV)

Most of the time, there aren't enough people in the kitchen. Yet, although the kitchen is a great place to serve, it's a poor place to live. That's the problem. Some people spend their whole lives in the kitchen. Some never leave it—maybe because of a misguided sense of duty, maybe because of feelings of inferiority. Whatever the reason, they feel they deserve recognition and hope people will notice their sacrifice. Like Martha, they abuse the kitchen.

Although the kitchen is a great place to serve, it's a poor place to live.

There Are Other Rooms in the House!

There's a living room. There's a bedroom for rest and sleep. There's a garage where you park the car, store things, and collect garbage. There's a workroom where chores are done and projects are finished. There's even a playroom for "re-creation."

By all means, shoulder the responsibility that is yours. But, like Mary, choose the best part. Balance your life. Spend quality time with the Master.

What Impresses Jesus?

Jesus yearns for intimacy with his people. Mary listened intently to Jesus; he likes that. He's impressed with spontaneous acts of love. It was Mary who anointed Jesus' feet with an expensive bottle of perfume (see John 12:3). The disciples were critical. It wasn't a practical thing to do. Judas even suggested that the perfume should have been sold and the money given to the poor. But Jesus was impressed with Mary's frivolous act of love. He's still impressed today when his people lavishly pour their love and praise upon him. Sometimes, we must realize that the practical thing isn't always the right thing.

Scripture says, "Enoch walked with God; then he was no more, because God took him away" (Gen. 5:24). A little boy once told the story better. He said, "Enoch and God were good friends. They often took long walks together. Sometimes they lost all track of time. One day they had walked and talked for hours. Enoch looked up and said, 'God it's getting late. I'd better head for home.' God said, 'We're closer to my house than yours. Why don't you just come home with me?' And so Enoch went home with God!" As you can see, Enoch's personal worship and devotion impressed God.

CHAPTER THIRTEEN

There Are Lots of Things to Do Outside the Kitchen!

Smell the roses. Watch a sunset or a sunrise! Really take in and appreciate God's beautiful world. We had about forty of our singles visit our cabin on Fort Gibson Lake. Our deck has a gorgeous view of the water as the sun sets behind the hills on the other side. I had them all stand with me and watch that marvelous act of God. As the reddish orange ball of blazing magnificence slowly disappeared and threw its fingers of beauty through the clouds, we sang the beautiful hymn by Stuart K. Hine "How Great Thou Art." What a time we had!

Play with a child. Making a living is not as important as making a life. Some parents confuse being good providers with being good parents. Kids don't need things; they need *you*! They don't need toys, they need *time!* Remember that bumper sticker, the one that said "Practice Random Acts of Kindness; Senseless Deeds of Beauty!"

Get in tune with God. Get in tune with his nature. Get in tune with his Word, his church, and his people. Get to know his values and priorities, his lifestyle and promises! If you're a Martha, I salute you. Hang in there with duty. Be a servant. Shoulder your responsibility. But for God's sake . . . now and then . . . get out of the kitchen!

Life Is a Terminal Disease

While speaking to some teachers at Fountainhead Lodge in El Reno, Oklahoma, I met Karen Bullock, who shared her inspirational story with me and gave me permission to use an essay she had written.

Karen's husband had become a victim of Hodgkin's disease while in Vietnam. Later, he developed heart trouble. He had to have bypass surgery and finally a transplant. His health problems had become a financial, emotional, and physical burden on the family. A so-called friend advised Karen to leave him and get on with her life. Karen shot back, "The difference between you and me is I know life is a terminal disease!" Each day is precious to Karen and her husband.

They don't take anything for granted. They accept each day as a loving gift from God. They always kiss good-bye; they always kiss hello! Because, as Karen says, "We never know when it might be the last one!" She says they're careful not to let little tragedies sidetrack them, and they try to live each day to the fullest.

Karen wrote the following essay:

Hugs from God

I live for them: those small, simple, unexpected events that give me a finer vision of this land and of myself. I collect them and hide them within the secret places of myself. They are moments of renewal and strength. And as I drift through these memories pressed in the pages of my soul, I can recall . . .

The feel of bare feet on sweet, summer grass that changes into a soft, thick pallet of moss;

The shock of a spring-fed creek, mud oozing between my toes, and bottom creatures tickling my feet;

The sight of American avocets as they fly away in black and white tuxedos with the style and grace of ballroom dancers;

The startling beauty of a golden thread of sunlight that stitches rain-depleted thunder clouds to a bruised, pink dawn sky;

The smell of crisp, autumn mornings while sitting beneath an old cottonwood and bathing in a shower of brightly colored leaves with each fresh, chilled breeze;

The joyous yodeling of a chorus of coyotes across the prairie at early dusk;

Life Is a Terminal Disease

The feel of rough, cold tree bark scratching my cheek as I
press my ear against the trunk to hear the spring sap
rush to the sun-gathering leaves;

The sight of a hesitant doe as it cautiously tiptoes across
a dusty road and bounds over a fence with less effort
than it takes me to skip rope;

The sharp, crisp odor of ozone generated by a lightning-
filled sky;

The persistent pleading of parent kingbirds as they teach
a hesitant fledgling to fly;

The red splash of sumac mingled with the brilliant
golden yellow ragweed in an abandoned field;

The musty smell of decayed leaves on the forest floor;

The stark silhouette of a great horned-owl as it roosts in
the bare branches of a tree;

The cold, sweet taste of frost-ripened persimmon picked
straight from the tree on a crisp, fall morning;

The sharp, well-defined, black "V" of geese flying against
the backdrop of a reddened sky;

The sight of fog tendrils winding around green gold
heads of wheat on a rainy, still morning;

The captivating sight of sparkling, white diamond stars
on a black velvet sky;

And the sharp crunch of ice-covered grass on a cold winter's day.

These small adventures catch in my throat as the earth
reaches out to grab me in a giant, tight embrace and time

holds still for that split moment when I know this creation—this space was designed especially for me. During these times, I fear even the simple act of breathing will wipe it away like a giant tornado. But I have found if I inhale deeply, these brief, impassioned scenes are captured by my breath and incorporated like oxygen into my cells, becoming part of me, never to be surrendered to oblivion, ready to be recalled in a needy moment. I call them "Hugs from God."

I Don't Mean to Be Morbid!

This title, "Life Is a Terminal Disease," can easily be taken literally. Many people today are pessimistic, neurotic, and negative. I saw one guy with a tattoo on his arm that said "Born to Go to Hell!" A college student once wrote, "Life is the penalty you pay for the crime of being born." One pessimist said, "If I inherited one thousand acres of pumpkins, they'd outlaw Halloween." And you know that famous line from *Hee-Haw,* "If it weren't for bad luck, I'd have no luck at all!"

Someone said, "Let a smile be your umbrella!" The other guy said, "I did and got beastly wet!" Someone else said, "Cheer up, things could get worse!" And the response came, "I did, and it did!"

This title simply means life is too short to spend it being depressed. We're only here for a little while. Make the most of it. Live life to the full. The Bible says, "All men are like grass, and all their glory is like the flowers of the field; the grass withers and the flowers fall, but the word of the Lord stands forever" (1 Pet. 1:24–25).

So remember two things. "Don't sweat the small stuff!" and "It's all small stuff!"

Jesus Wants Us to Grab the Gusto

A beer commercial once said, "You only go around once in life. You've got to grab all the gusto you can get!" I'm not sure the brewery knew the slogan was from Scripture. But that's what the Bible says:

> I have come that they may have life, and have it to the full. (John 10:10)

> This day I call heaven and earth as witnesses against you that I have set before you life and death, blessings and curses. Now choose life. (Deut. 30:19)

The first-century Christians were full of joy and happiness, and they spent a lot of time rejoicing:

> They . . . ate together with glad and sincere hearts, praising God and enjoying the favor of all the people. (Acts 2:46–47)

> Philip went down to a city in Samaria and proclaimed the Christ there. . . . So there was great joy in that city. (Acts 8:5, 8)

> The fruit of the Spirit is love, joy, peace, patience, kindness, goodness, faithfulness, gentleness and self-control. (Gal. 5:22–23)

And don't forget that marvelous verse, "Be joyful always" (1 Thess. 5:16).

Why should Christians be joyful? We are forgiven. We have a father, a fellowship, a family, and a future that is unparalleled!

CHAPTER FOURTEEN

Live One Day at a Time

Most members of Alcoholics Anonymous carry a coin in their pocket with the inscription "Live One Day at a Time." It reminds them to live in "day tight" compartments. I have a friend named Cotton who remembers it this way. Before he goes to sleep each night, he throws his shoes as far under the bed as he can. In the morning, while he's down on his knees trying to reach his shoes, he asks God to help him stay sober just for that day! He has stretched that philosophy into several years of sobriety. Have you ever heard about the clock that was told it must tick 31,536,000 times a year. It was about to die of heart failure (if clocks have hearts). Then it was told that it would only have to tick one tick at a time.

Enjoying the Disease

Karen and her husband have decided to enjoy the disease! This doesn't mean they like pain. It simply means that into every life some rain must fall. They accept the rain, mix it with the sun, and make beautiful rainbows.

Lots of good things don't last, but we enjoy them anyway— books, movies, trips, vacations, youth, health, and life! Those having the most fun know life is terminal. They've decided to emphasize the positive, magnify the beautiful, and take everything else in stride.

Claudette Jones was dying of cancer. She carried her oxygen bottle with her everywhere she went. One day, she told her husband, "I think I'll go parasailing!" He said, "You're out of your mind. It's too dangerous!" Laughingly, she replied, "What's it going to do? Kill me?" And she went!

Life Is a Terminal Disease

Mary Cook, one of my dear friends, was also dying of cancer. When they told her, she said, "Good, now I'll eat all the Sonic hamburgers I want!" Before, they had been taboo on her diet. We are all terminal, so get on with life! Live it to the fullest!

Life was meant to be lived. Someone once said, "Only 5 percent of the people make things happen. Eighty percent watch things happen. And 15 percent have no idea what is happening!" I choose to be in the 5 percent! How about you?

Some lose spontaneity and become pessimistic and negative with age. Grab life by the horns. Enjoy your relationships. Spend quality time with your spouse, your kids, your grandkids, and your friends. Enjoy the people of God. The church reminds me of a sign I saw outside Milford, Texas, that read,

Milford, Texas
City of 750 Friendly People
And Two or Three Old Grouches!

Get out and travel. This is a beautiful world. See your state and your nation. Go overseas, take cruises, and see the world's wonders.

Jump on your motorcycle, get in your car or van, catch a plane or ship, but get out there. Spend your kids' inheritance money, it'll probably save them from squabbling over your will!

Emphasize the positive, magnify the beautiful, and take everything else in stride.

Start an exciting spiritual walk with God now! Discover God, don't manufacture him. Read his book. Give him your life. Discover the beauty of his way!

Someday We'll Celebrate the Cure!

We won't always be terminal; one day we'll be *eternal*. Heaven is going to be beyond our wildest dreams.

Heaven Will Be a Release

We will be set free from this frail old body. The Bible says, "[God] will wipe every tear from [our] eyes. There will be no more death or mourning or crying or pain, for the old order of things has passed away" (Rev. 21:4).

Heaven Will Be a Reunion

Christians never have to say good-bye for the last time. Heaven is the mother of all reunions. Paul writes, "For what is our hope, our joy, or the crown in which we will glory in the presence of our Lord Jesus when he comes? Is it not you?" (1 Thess. 2:19).

Heaven Is "Face to Face"

"We know that when he appears, we shall be like him, for we shall see him as he is" (1 John 3:2). It reminds me of the beautiful song by Mrs. Frank A. Breck:

> Face to face with Christ my Savior,
> Face to face what will it be,
> When with rapture I behold Him,
> Jesus Christ who died for me?

Red Skelton said his father told him, "Don't take life too seriously; you'll never get out of it alive!" So grab the gusto today . . . and every day! And be drawn by the gusto forever!

What Makes America Great?

Too many Americans take our marvelous country for granted. The Fourth of July rolls around, and they think more about what they'll pack in the cooler to take to the fireworks display than they do about what the fireworks are commemorating. Many citizens can't answer even the simplest questions about the country they claim to love: What happened on July 4, 1776? Who was the first president? Which president freed the slaves? Name the three branches of government. Who is the chief justice? Who becomes president if both the president and vice president die? Who is the governor of your state and the mayor of your city? Who wrote most of the Constitution? What freedoms are guaranteed in the Bill of Rights?

For patriots, it's easy to be discouraged when so many citizens seem apathetic toward the country we call home. But my spirits received a boost when author Stephen Covey wrote in *USA Weekend* (July 4, 1997) about a recent survey of American citizens, which found that the following values are still alive in America. They are the ideals that gave birth to our nation, and they are still the beliefs that make America great.

- 95 percent believe freedom must be tempered with personal responsibility.
- 89 percent believe it's their responsibility to help those less fortunate.
- 86 percent believe that, despite our mobile society, family ties are more important than ever.
- 83 percent believe America is the greatest nation in the world.
- 81 percent believe a spiritual and religious belief is essential to a fulfilling life.
- 80 percent believe personal responsibility has more to do with success than does personal circumstance.
- 79 percent believe that people who work hard in this nation are most likely to succeed.
- 76 percent believe the government should help those who cannot care for themselves.
- 70 percent believe that, in general, children raised in two-parent families fare better than those raised in single-parent families.

A Refreshing Look at America

We cling to these foundational truths when the media give us a narrower view of our country. Headlines scream that homosexuals are coming out of the closet and flaunting their lifestyles in public parades. Some states are considering acceptance of same-sex marriages. Athletes are taking illegal drugs, practicing group sex, raping women, and biting chunks out of their opponents' ears. Couples are living together without marriage. There's an exploding problem of child pornography, sexual harassment, and domestic abuse. Adultery, casual sex, violence, and filthy language fill TV screens, movies, and novels.

When such topics fill the airways and the newspapers, we need to look with renewed pride at Mr. and Mrs. Average America, that quiet, nondescript couple who still clings to morality, honesty, and integrity. We need to remember that most Americans still keep their promises, pay their debts, and honor their commitments. The majority of Americans are still people of character and ethics. We must cling to those facts, even when they don't make the news.

Actually, in an ironic way, those headlines that describe incidents of crime, corruption, racism, and violence should offer a sense of encouragement, because something is news only when it a departure from the norm. Vile actions make headlines because they are not what the average American is doing. Instead the terrible story being reported makes the front page because it is unusual, the exception to the rule.

> We need to look with renewed pride at Mr. and Mrs. Average America.

When you feel a sense of gloom and doom creeping in as you listen to the evening news, keep this fact in mind: America is still basically the opposite of the top stories on the newscast!

A Patriot's View of This Great Country

I admit to being a card-carrying, native-born, dyed-in-the-wool American, a veteran of the Korean War. I'm an unabashed patriot. I still get tears in my eyes when a crowd sings "The Star-Spangled Banner." I press my right hand to my heart as the color guard leads the parade down Main Street and Old Glory passes by. In front of our home in Oklahoma the Stars and Stripes flies proudly from a flagpole, dipping reverently to half-staff to honor fallen heroes on appropriate occasions.

I love America—not that other nations have no appeal for me. I've traveled through more than twenty-five countries, and I've learned that our American culture is not the only way to do things. There are plenty of good lessons we can learn from other people and their customs. And much of the world seems willing to learn from us. The respect shown us by other nationalities imposes both honor and duty. Every American, from our president down to the lowest tourist, has a responsibility to leave a favorable impression on those who look up to us. I do my best to represent America favorably as I travel, and I've enjoyed the people I've met and the experiences I've had in other lands. But I'm always glad to be back in "the land of the free and the home of the brave."

Yes, I love my country. But I know how easy it is these days to think the United States is going down the tubes—sliding down the gutter into moral and cultural ruin. When such thoughts threaten me with discouragement, I cling to the facts—remembering that current trends are far more important than the isolated abnormalities making the headlines. And the trends that are occurring are encouraging indeed. They make us aware of our great opportunities to honor God and perpetuate God's blessings on our country.

Americans Are Going Back to Church

The most encouraging trend is that America is returning to its roots. Our early presidents and leaders were God-fearing, Bible-believing, church-going men and women! Congress was opened and closed with Bible reading and prayer. God's help was sought in the affairs of state. Our Constitution was designed to protect our freedom *of* religion, not our freedom *from* religion.

America was founded as a God-fearing nation. But somewhere along the way, we lost sight of the elements that made it so: vibrant churches where God is honored, Christ is preached, and hope is given. Now things are starting to change. Researcher George Barna recently identified seven trends affecting church growth that are occurring as America approaches the third millennium:

- More people are attending church.
- There is an increased emphasis on the family.
- Americans are on a quest for lasting relationships.
- Mass-media ministries are declining.
- A change is occurring in the support base of the church.
- Polarization is increasing between evangelical and ecumenical movements.
- Government is becoming more involved in church affairs.

The trends also show that a moral and spiritual revival is taking place in our country. Churches that are aware of these trends and are responding to them appropriately are growing impressively. These are Bible-believing churches that teach the Word as a revelation from God and of God. Within these congregations, the same values that made our nation great are being taught and nurtured. Here, individuals gain spiritual strength, and healthy families are honored and supported. The values held by such churches are demonstrated by the mission statement of the church where I preached for twenty-six years. It still reads, "We are a family, dedicated to Christ and his Word and led by the Holy Spirit. We demonstrate God's love by taking care of each other, building strong families, and reaching out as Christ to our community."

Churches that share this kind of focus show such characteristics as:

- A strong belief and commitment to God and the Bible
- A strong belief in nuclear families that are committed to God and to each other
- A strong belief in personal responsibility, hard work, honesty, integrity, and ethics
- A strong concern for those less fortunate and a desire to help them stand on their own feet again
- A strong belief in the rights and convictions of others even when they differ from our own
- A strong belief that people have the power to shape their own lives and decide their own destinies

Americans Know They Need God

In order to grow, churches today must speak to Americans' renewed need to know God. They must rise above the "issues" mentality, stop "majoring in minors," and focus instead on the simple but life-changing facts of the gospel. I quote my good friend Victor Knowles, who says, "Any issue the Peruvian housewife cannot understand cannot be essential to salvation!"

Churches must refocus on Jesus Christ, remembering that Christianity is much more than a system of rituals. It is the worship of a

Person. Respect for Jesus as Lord brings with it respect for his Word, his way, and his church. The apostle Paul put it succinctly: "When I came to you, brothers, I did not come with eloquence or superior wisdom as I proclaimed to you the testimony about God. For I resolved to know nothing while I was with you except Jesus Christ and him crucified" (1 Cor. 2:1–2).

God Bless America

America and its churches still have many problems. But the blessings far exceed the curses. The opportunities are light-years ahead of the obstacles. The truth is, you and I live smack in the middle of the best country in the world. God bless you! God bless the churches of our nation! And especially, God bless America!

Peace, Be Still

Then he got into the boat and his disciples followed him. Without warning, a furious storm came up on the lake, so that the waves swept over the boat. But Jesus was sleeping. The disciples went and woke him, saying, "Lord, save us! We're going to drown!"

He replied, "You of little faith, why are you so afraid?" Then he got up and rebuked the winds and the waves, and it was completely calm."

The men were amazed and asked, "What kind of man is this? Even the winds and the waves obey him!" (Matt. 8:23–27)

This passage describes a wonderful glimpse into Jesus' everyday life. He had just finished the Sermon on the Mount (Matt. 5–7). Then followed three quick healings—a man with leprosy, a centurion's servant, and Peter's mother-in-law. The Bible says, "Many who were demon-possessed were brought to him, and he drove out the spirits with a word and healed all the sick" (Matt. 8:16).

Then he went back to teaching the cost of discipleship: Foxes and birds have places to sleep, he said, but the Son of Man has nowhere to lay his head. Persecution and deprivation are in store for those who choose to follow me, he warned, but they will find peace.

On the Sea of Galilee

Then Jesus, exhausted, turned aside to escape the crowd for a while. It had been a long, hard day. With a few disciples, he boarded a little boat, and they pushed out from shore. The boat's gentle rocking was peaceful, and the breeze was nice. It was one of his few chances to escape the rigors of the day. Soon the Lord was fast asleep.

Galilee is noted for sudden storms. A glassy sea can become a raging tempest in a few moments. This storm hit as Jesus was sleeping in the stern of the boat. Waves broke over the bow, and the boat was nearly swamped. The disciples were terrified. In their fear they cried out, "Jesus, don't you care if we drown?"

The men's cries awakened Jesus. As he stretched, he asked, as though puzzled, "Why are you afraid? Where's your faith?" And then he turned toward the water and uttered three simple words: "Peace, be still!" (Mark 4:39 KJV). The wind immediately died down, and the sea was completely calm.

I've been on the Sea of Galilee as a tourist on a boat with a motor. The memories of Scripture flooded my soul as our little boat rose and fell with the rolling waves. We shut off the engines and sang this

Peace Be Still

powerful song by Horatio R. Palmer:

> Master, the tempest is raging!
> The billows are tossing high!
> The sky is o'ershadowed with blackness,
> No shelter or help is nigh;
> Carest Thou not that we perish?
> How canst Thou lie asleep,
> When each moment so madly is threat'ning
> A grave in the angry deep?
> The winds and the waves shall obey Thy will,
> Peace, be still!

On that day when Jesus slept in the boat, the wind and waves on the sea were furious. The little boat bobbed and rolled in the storm. Water coursed over the deck, drenching the men. At any moment the disciples expected to be swept overboard and lost. Terrified, they fairly screamed the question: "Don't you care if we drown?"

Their query was understandable. They wanted to know about Jesus' ability and dependability: Can you do anything about this problem, Lord? *Will* you?

The question is still understandable today. Can Jesus really help us in the storms we face in life? Does he care enough to do anything about our troubles?

As the rain fell and the wind howled that afternoon, Jesus countered with a question of his own: "Why are you worried?" He wanted them to know that as long as they were with

Can Jesus really help us in the storms we face in life? Does he care enough to do anything about our troubles?

him, things were going to be all right. He still wants us to know that.

The Bible and Peace

God's peace runs like a silver thread through the Scriptures:

> The Lord bless you and keep you; the Lord make his face to shine upon you and be gracious to you; the Lord turn his face toward you and give you peace. (Num. 6:24–26)

> I will lie down and sleep in peace, for you alone, O Lord, make me dwell in safety. (Ps. 4:8)

> Great peace have they who love your law, and nothing can make them stumble. (Ps. 119:165)

> Better a dry crust of bread with peace and quiet than a house full of feasting, with strife. (Prov. 17:1)

> I will make a covenant of peace with them; it will be an everlasting covenant. I will establish them and increase their numbers, and I will put my sanctuary among them forever. (Ezek. 37:26)

> Peace I leave with you; my peace I give you. I do not give to you as the world gives. Do not let your hearts be troubled and do not be afraid. (John 14:27)

Our Search for Peace

I wonder how many of you remember the significance of September 2, 1945. It was the end of World War II, the day the newspaper headlines anounced, "Peace Declared!" Recently I saw, in a Seattle dry dock, the very ship on which America accepted the unconditional surrender of Japan to end the war.

The treaty was signed on that ship, but world peace didn't last. Since then ferocious wars and bloody battles have raged in Korea, Vietnam, Granada, Kuwait, Bosnia, Croatia, Cambodia, Ireland, and other places many of us had never even heard of until a few years ago.

On the home front, we've had the New York Trade Center bombing and the infamous bombing of the Murrah Building in Oklahoma City. We look for news of peace in the newspapers. Instead, we read of crime, killing, raping, and robbing. We look for it in our neighborhoods but instead find signs announcing the community's "Neighborhood Watch" and hear tales of breaking and entering. We hope for peace in our homes, but too often they are scenes of neglect, abuse, and domestic violence. "For Sale" signs on lawns often mean the homes' occupants have recently divorced and are selling off the assets.

We look for peace in our schools, thinking surely we'll find it in the places where our young people are being trained for life. Instead we are shocked to see metal detectors where knives and guns are collected from children. Violence in classrooms, rest rooms, and playgrounds leaves us perplexed in our search for peace.

Ah, but certainly we'll find peace in our churches, where God's children gather! And we do hear peace, love, unity, and harmony preached from their pulpits. But sometimes the words are nothing but a veneer of pious pretension hiding a structure weakened by division and strife, politics and tumult.

We crave smooth sailing in life but find little of it. There are storms building around us everywhere we turn, threatening sickness and sorrow, crisis and calamity. We're going to experience disappointment, pain, setback, separation, and, oh yes, there's going to be death. We crave peace but cannot find it.

The Promise of Peace

We will do just about anything in this quest for peace. Some of us even use pills, needles, and alcohol to ease our pain. We turn up the noise to drown out our fears. But real peace eludes us. We form alliances, make promises, and give up everything to obtain peace. Seeking it, we'll run one way and then the other to anything or anyone—until finally we find the only One who can provide it.

Real Peace Is a Person

I remember the day when my desk was piled high, deadlines were closing in on me, committee meetings were scheduled, and problems were brewing. (There are always problems brewing somewhere in a growing, thousand-member church.) I was stressed, ready to throw up my hands and throw in the towel. My hands clutched at the tightness in my chest as I tried to choose between Zantac and Tagamet. And then it hit me: Peace isn't a pill. Real peace is a Person!

Jesus was the "Prince of Peace" (Isa. 9:6). He was sent "to shine on those living in darkness and in the shadow of death, to guide our feet into the path of peace" (Luke 1:79). When Jesus was born, the angels sang, "Glory to God in the highest, and on earth peace, good will toward men!" (Luke 2:14 KJV). When Jesus appeared to his disciples after his resurrection, he said, "Peace be with you!" (John 20:19). The apostles preached, "You know the message God sent to the people of Israel, telling the good news of peace through Jesus Christ, who is Lord of all" (Acts 10:36).

Nineteen of the twenty-seven books in the New Testament begin with the greeting "Grace and peace to you through our Lord Jesus Christ." Paul declared of Jesus, "For he himself is our peace, who has made the two one and has destroyed the barrier, the dividing wall of hostility" (Eph. 2:14). And Paul wrote, "The peace of God, which transcends all understanding, will guard your hearts and your minds in Christ Jesus" (Phil. 4:7).

Peace in Jesus is not something we earn through hard work or win by defeating our competitors. It is simply a matter of decision, priority, attitude, and lifestyle. The Bible tells us to "submit to God and be at peace with him" (Job 22:21).

Four Traits of God's Peace

Psalm 23 is probably one of the best-known pieces of literature in the world. Surely it's the one of most memorized and quoted passages of all Scripture. From it we learn four things about the peace found in Jesus Christ.

1. God's Peace Is Emancipating

In Christ we find freedom from guilt, freedom from worry, freedom to be who we are, and freedom to start all over again! "The Lord is my Shepherd, I shall not be in want," David sang. A little boy was having trouble memorizing the Twenty-third Psalm. He made several pitiful tries at remembering those few verses. Finally, in desperation, he blurted out, "The Lord is my Shepherd . . . why should I worry?" He had it right on target! God's peace is freeing!

Jesus was always saying, "Don't be afraid!"

We want to answer, Well, why not? The wind is howling, the waves are about to swallow us up, and death is circling above us. Why shouldn't we be afraid?

Because, he answers, "I will never leave you nor forsake you" (Heb. 13:5 NKJV). And "[I] will keep in perfect peace him whose mind is steadfast, because he trusts in [me]" (Isa. 26:3).

2. God's Peace Is Exclusive

David said, "I will fear no evil, for you are with me" (Ps. 23:4). God is personal. Remember that old hymn, "My God and I walk through the fields together. We walk and talk as good friends should and do"? Thomas called him, "my Lord and my God" (John 20:28). Peace is only promised to God's people. Jesus promised to never leave us alone. And it's a good thing, because he also said, "Apart from me you can do nothing" (John 15:5).

3. God's Peace Is Energizing

We hear David say, "He restores my soul" (Ps. 23:3). Have you ever been so scared you could not move, no matter how hard you tried? Fear paralyzes us, but God's peace restores our strength. It gives us energy, vitality, creativity, and spontaneity. Scripture says, "May the God who gives endurance and encouragement give you a spirit of unity among yourselves as you follow Christ Jesus, so that with one heart and mouth you may glorify the God and Father of our Lord Jesus Christ" (Rom. 15:5–6).

4. God's Peace Is Enduring

How deep is this peace he gives us? It is as deep as valley of the shadow of death. Yes, even there, "I will fear no evil, for you are with me" (Ps 23:4).

Peace Be Still

How long is this peace? It endures throughout eternity. As David said, "I will dwell in the house of the LORD forever" (v. 6).

A woman I knew had been a Christian all her life. On her deathbed she struggled, no doubt, with what to say. She hated good-byes, as we all do. But she knew God's promises and believed them, so she knew this good-bye wasn't forever. With her last breath, she turned to her grieving son at her bedside and simply said, "See ya!" She knew Christians never say good-bye for the last time.

Sometimes we don't know where to turn. But, thank God, we always know to *whom* to turn. Jesus cares! And he gives us peace!

17

A Real Hall of Famer

You want to hear a real love story? Here's one out of the second chapter of Philippians. Jesus Christ was God. Yet as he looked down over a world of sin and sinners, his heart went out to them. He left his sovereignty as God and clothed himself with flesh. He became a man, yet he was not just a man; nor was he a VIP with an impressive title. He became a servant.

He submitted himself to death by crucifixion. He died for us! Then his Father raised him from the dead and exalted him above every name. He promised that someday every tongue would confess Jesus' name and every knee would bow before him—some of them too late to be saved.

Now *that's* what I call a love story! Here's another one:

CHAPTER SEVENTEEN

Scene One: Seventeen-year-old Daniel Huffman, a student athlete in Rossville, Illinois—with fourteen hundred people, hardly a speck on the map—118 miles south of Chicago. Here was a young man who was really on his way. Six-foot-two, 275 pounds, Daniel liked football, and he was good at it too—really good! Daniel was the "screamer" on the team, a one-man pep rally. He thrived on "two-a-day" practices. His coach said he literally swarmed opposing running backs, slamming them to the ground before they knew what had hit them.

Daniel was also an honor student with an A-plus average, a member of the school chorus, the class vice president, and a writer of poetry. He was a shot putter on the track team and held a part-time job at a discount store in town. He wanted to make his senior year at Rossville High School a real doozie. And he did, but not in the way you might think.

With his size and talent there was little doubt among area football coaches that he would one day sign with the pros. He was headed in that direction, to be sure. But Daniel made a dumb decision. Or maybe it was a brilliant decision. I'll leave it to you to decide.

Scene Two: Enter Daniel's sixty-year-old grandmother, Shirlee Allison. She played a key role in Daniel's hall-of-fame status. You see, Shirlee had diabetes. She was legally blind and considered a terminal case.

At this point one of the strange twists in the story comes into play. You see, Daniel's mother had left the family when Daniel was four. His father remarried. Daniel had a thirteen-year-old sister, Kristina, and their relationship with their new stepmother wasn't good. So after seventh grade, Daniel and Kristina moved to Florida to live with their mom. That didn't work out either, so they both ended up living with their grandparents.

Daniel loved his grandmother. He did her dishes. He folded the laundry. He became Shirlee's eyes, helping her walk and reading her mail to her. Daniel was her strength when his grandfather went through quintuple heart bypass surgery. Shirlee said, "Sometimes we raised them; sometimes they raised us!" Daniel credited his grandparents with keeping him out of drugs and other trouble.

He had a lot of friends, and he was always willing to lend a hand or a listening ear. A classmate, Lisa Masengale, said, "He'd do anything for us. He writes me poetry when I'm down. He can always make me laugh!"

Daniel and his grandmother ended up being kind of an "odd couple." He was getting physically bigger every day while Shirlee seemed to be disappearing before his very eyes. Her kidneys failed, and she had to go on regular dialysis. Her condition got steadily worse as her muscles atrophied, her heart enlarged, and her blood pressure got dangerously low. Her doctor said many people could live for years on dialysis, but Shirlee wasn't one of them. Her only hope was a kidney transplant.

Scene Three: Daniel began to read everything he could find on kidney disease, dialysis, transplants, you name it. He talked to Shirlee's doctors and learned that she might have hope of a near-normal life if they could just locate a kidney for a transplant.

Daniel had himself typed. He was a match.

He didn't have to do it. His grandmother didn't ask him to. And he knew the risks. To give his sixty-year-old grandmother one of his kidneys would mean the end of his football career. In fact, it would end his involvement in contact sports *forever.* One hit might mean his life. He also learned that eight people a day die while waiting for an available organ.

CHAPTER SEVENTEEN

Daniel was sitting with his grandmother at the Burger King when he made up his mind. He suddenly blurted out, "I want you to take my kidney!"

"Absolutely not," Shirlee responded. "The thought of you giving up football makes me sick!"

But Daniel was adamant. "Gran," he said, "you always taught me to stand up for what I believe. That's what I'm doing. You're taking my kidney!" He was fairly shouting.

His mother was against it. She even tried to stop it, pleading that he was a minor and didn't have the right to make such a decision. Daniel would turn eighteen soon, but he argued, "Gran might die before then."

He found a doctor and a hospital that would do the transplant. The operation was scheduled.

Scene Four: Shirlee Allison is doing well. "I have the kidney of a seventeen-year-old football player. I just hope I don't get the uncontrollable urge to go out and tackle somebody!" she joked recently. And Daniel? Well, a lot of wonderful things have happened to Daniel. He had to quit the football team, of course. But they didn't quit him. The players insisted he wear his jersey to every game. He even went to practice whenever he wasn't working, and at the games he led the crowd in cheering for his team.

Doctors know that Daniel's good kidney has grown almost twice its original size. They haven't figured out a way to measure his heart.

His story is getting out. *Sports Illustrated* did a special on him, and Illinois Governor Jim Edgar wrote to say how proud he was of Daniel. Both local and national TV picked up the story. Soon, a nation would know about the boy who gave up what could have been a lucrative future to save his grandmother's life.

And the football team? Well, it went three-and-six without Daniel as defensive back. But they won their last game 28 to 3. And near the end of that game they did an amazing thing. They called Daniel onto the field with twenty-four seconds left to play. They had him line up twenty yards behind the line of scrimmage. Then the quarterback took the snap and dropped to his knee to end the game. Daniel, twenty yards back, raised his arms in a V for victory. Later he said, "It was the single best moment in my life."

Epilogue

It's a great story, isn't it? And I'm naive enough to believe we can learn something from it. Sometimes the people of God need stories like this to remind us how to treat one another. What tremendous value there is in us, in our fellow human beings, and in relationships of love—not only in our earthly families but in God's family, the church. When we forget this value, bad things happen—grudges build, struggles for power erupt, politics get ugly, church members fight, and congregations split.

When the herdsmen of Abraham and Lot quarreled over pasture rights and water holes, the relationship between uncle and nephew was in jeopardy. Abraham pulled it back into perspective. "Let's not have any quarreling between you and me, or between your herdsmen and mine, for we are brothers," he said (Gen. 13:8). And then he suggested that Lot pick any direction to move his estate. Abraham would take what was left. There was a man who understood peace and family.

The story of Daniel and his grandmother pulls us back to what really matters—and it isn't football or youth or personal gain. It's love, the greatest thing in the world (see 1 Cor. 13:13). The story pulls us to a higher dimension of thinking about our value system and our entire lifestyle. Suddenly we see that real success is loving someone worth loving, holding on to something that's big enough to hold you in return.

> Real success is loving someone worth loving, holding on to something that's big enough to hold you in return.

In today's world of shallow self-centeredness, the masses value things and devalue people. Relationships take a backseat to riches. But Someone said a long time ago, "It is more blessed to give than receive" (Acts 20:35). And, "Greater love has no one than this, that he lay down his life for his friends" (John 15:13).

God gave more than a kidney. He gave his one and only Son.

Jesus gave more than great teaching. The lesson the Lord shared is indelibly written on a blood-stained cross outside Jerusalem. He died that you and I might live.

As the story of Daniel and Shirlee moves you to tears, let the story of Jesus move you to commitment and salvation.

Whoever

The most beautiful part of the verse we call the "golden text" of the Bible is the simple word *whoever.* Think about it: "For God so loved the world that he gave his one and only Son, that *whoever* believes in him shall not perish but have eternal life" (John 3:16).

The word means anyone—any and every person on earth—can come to the Father. The invitation is totally unrestricted and all-encompassing all. No one is left out, held back, or unqualified. That's what Jesus meant when he said *whoever.* He meant you and me. No matter who we are, no matter what we've done, we can come to him. Neither the size nor the number of our sins matters. We can come to him and find eternal life.

CHAPTER EIGHTEEN

Listen as the Bible soothes our hearts and soul with other texts exuding the beauty of the word *whoever:*

> *Whoever* listens to me will live in safety and be at ease, without fear of harm. (Prov. 1:33)

> *Whoever* trusts in the LORD is kept safe. (Prov. 29:25)

> *Whoever* acknowledges me before men, I will also acknowledge him before my Father in heaven. (Matt. 10:32)

> *Whoever* does the will of my Father in heaven is my brother and sister and mother. (Matt. 12:50)

> *Whoever* believes in him is not condemned, but *whoever* does not believe stands condemned already because he has not believed in the name of God's one and only Son. (John 3:18)

> *Whoever* believes in the Son has eternal life, but *whoever* rejects the Son will not see life, for God's wrath remains on him. (John 3:36)

> *Whoever* drinks the water I give him will never thirst. (John 4:14)

> *Whoever* hears my word and believes him who sent me has eternal life and will not be condemned; he has crossed over from death to life. (John 5:24)

> All [another word like *whoever*] that the Father gives me will come to me, and *whoever* comes to me I will never drive away. (John 6:37)

When Jesus spoke again to the people, he said, "I am the

light of the world. *Whoever* follows me will never walk in darkness, but will have the light of life." (John 8:12)

I am the gate; *whoever* enters through me will be saved. He will come in and go out and find pasture. (John 10:9)

Go into all the world and preach the good news to all creation. *Whoever* believes and is baptized will be saved, but whoever does not believe will be condemned. (Mark 16:15–16)

The Bible ends with this thought: "*Whoever* is thirsty, let him come; and *whoever* wishes, let him take the free gift of the water of life" (Rev. 22:17). The good news is that Jesus will take *anyone* in; he'll take *anyone* back. Even you and me.

Even a Five-Time Divorcee with a Live-in Lover

There is a marvelous story in John 4 that tells how Jesus "had" to go through Samaria (v. 4). He didn't have to, you know. Jewish roads led around Samaria because the Jews considered Samaritans low-class "half-breeds," little better than dogs—even worse than Gentiles. But Jesus would not travel a road paved with prejudice; he *had* to go through Samaria. There he encountered a Samaritan woman at Jacob's well. She was amazed that Jesus (a Jew) would talk to her (a Samaritan woman). Jesus asked for a drink and talked of water not from that well but water that would satisfy her forever.

When he instructed her to "Go, call your husband and come back" (v. 16), she answered, "I don't have a husband." Then Jesus, no doubt with a sympathetic smile, said, in effect, "I know you don't. You've had five husbands. And now you have a live-in lover." He did not say this to condemn her but to let her know he knew all things.

She was someone no upstanding church congregation would want. Yet she was included in Jesus' invitation to *whoever.*

Caught in the Act

Four chapters later, in John 8:1–11, there is another wonderful story. A woman had been caught in the very act of adultery. Usually when a woman is caught in adultery the man who is with her is "caught" too. But in Jewish prejudice this woman's partner wasn't even mentioned. The Jewish leaders focused only on the woman's transgression, noting that "the Law says this woman should be stoned to death." Then they asked Jesus, "What do you say?"

The Bible tells us they said this only to trap Jesus and have a reason for putting him to death. Jesus scribbled in the dirt as they questioned him. Then he arose and spoke to them, and his reply was phenomenal: "Let the one who is without sin throw the first rock," he said. Then he stooped back down to write upon the sand some more. Hearing his words, the reality of their own sins dawned on the Jewish leaders, and the sting of their own arrogance overwhelmed them. One by one they left.

The woman suddenly found herself standing there alone, bewildered by the situation. After a moment Jesus looked up. "Where are your accusers?" he asked.

"They're gone," the woman replied.

Jesus smiled and said, "I don't condemn you either. Go home, and don't let anyone use you anymore." The adulterous woman was included in the Lord's *whoever.*

Even Murderers

The second chapter of Acts is the pivotal chapter of the Bible. Everything that happened before it points there. Everything that happened after that time points back to it.

By this point, Jesus had been savagely crucified. Three days later the tomb had been found empty; the body was missing. Now the hottest issue of the day was, "What happened to the body of Jesus?" No one dared talk openly about it, and few allowed their minds to even think, *What if he really was the Messiah?*

Then came the scene described in Acts 2. The people were in Jerusalem for Pentecost when suddenly they heard a sound like a violent wind. Tongues of fire danced over the heads of the apostles, and suddenly the disciples were speaking languages they didn't even know they knew! As you might imagine, this caused quite a stir. People gathered around the disciples, asking, "What does this mean?"

Then Peter stood up and addressed the crowd. The man they had nailed to the cross, he told them, really was the Son of God.

Now, what's the worst sin you could ever commit? What's the one sin that could never be forgiven, the one act that would put you forever beyond the grace of God? Wouldn't you imagine that it's murder, especially the murder of God's only Son? Realizing what they had done, the people were terrified. In their panic they cried out, "Men and brothers, what can we do?"

They probably expected Peter to say, "There's *nothing* you can do. You murderers! You killed God's Son, and he's comin' to get you!"

Instead, they heard the most incredible words: "Repent and be baptized, and you will be forgiven, indwelled by the Holy Spirit, and added as saved people to the church that was bought with the blood shed on that very cross!"

The Bible says the people—three thousand of them—gladly accepted Peter's advice and were baptized. Jesus included in *whoever* even his own murderers.

The Excluded Are Included

Paul wrote to the Corinthian Christians:

> Do you not know that the wicked will not inherit the king-dom of God? Do not be deceived: Neither the sexually immoral nor idolaters nor adulterers nor male prostitutes nor homosexual offenders nor thieves nor the greedy nor drunkards nor slanderers nor swindlers will inherit the king-dom of God. And that is what some of you were. But you were washed, you were sanctified, you were justified in the name of the Lord Jesus Christ and by the Spirit of our God. (1 Cor. 6:9–11)

Take a look at Paul's list of scoundrels. Some of the most immoral and despicable villains on earth are named on it, and Paul plainly states that these people will *not* go to heaven. But what if someone wants to remove his or her name from that infamous list? What if the worst of the worst chooses to turn to Jesus? Because of the gospel of Christ and the grace of God, they are all included in *whoever*.

What if the worst of the worst chooses to turn to Jesus?

Even You and I

I was preaching one Sunday night in an Oklahoma prison. It was a routine trip that I make four times a year. After I had preached this sermon on the word *whoever,* we sang a routine invitation song to encourage listeners to respond to Jesus. As we sang, an elderly man arose slowly from the back row and with difficulty hobbled toward the front.

He stood there, head bowed, until the song ended. Then, with tears in his eyes, he told me, "I was beaten regularly by my father when I was a child. He broke both my hips. He told me again and again that I was no good, that I'd never amount to anything, that I'd end up in prison! Well, here I am. But tonight I learned that God loves me. I realized I am included in that beautiful word *whoever.* And I want to surrender my life to him."

How beautiful it was to watch that man be baptized and start his new life in Christ that night.

Are you an alcoholic or a drug addict? You're included in *whoever!* Are you a thief convicted of armed robbery? Are you right now in jail because of crimes like these? You're in *whoever!* Are you an adulterer? Abuser? Homosexual? A molester or a prostitute? When Jesus said "whoever," he drew a circle around you to draw you in.

Has pornography got you in its clutches? Does gossip control your tongue? Has violence marred your soul? That little word *whoever* is your hope!

Are there secret sins in your life? Are sexual, moral, or emotional problems darkening your life and destroying your hope? Don't you understand? Because of that word *whoever* you can hope again. There is no sin, no time limit, that puts you out of the desire of God to include you in his marvelous love.

The good news I bring is that God wants everyone to be saved. All of us. Every one of us. Scripture tells us, "The Lord is . . . not willing that any should perish, but that all should come to repentance" (2 Pet. 3:9 KJV).

Surrender your life to Jesus now! Trust him as your Lord and Savior! Commit to him in repentance and baptism. Join in the fellowship and serve in his blood-bought church. And then write me and tell me you have done this. (Marvin Phillips Ministries, P.O. Box 691964, Tulsa, OK 74169)

Praise God for John 3:16! Praise God for *whoever*!

19

TGI2DAY

Everyone knows that TGIF means "Thank God it's Friday!" I recently saw a license plate that said "TGI2DAY." This message radiates with enthusiasm and optimism. You know someone with a license plate like this has to have a positive mental attitude. They feel good about life; they enjoy the moment and live in the *now!* TGI2DAY would make a great T-shirt logo but an even better way of life! Have you guessed what it means yet? Bursting with zest for life, it says, "Thank God it's today."

So many people live in the past. Do you know why old people talk so much about the "good old days?" Because that's all they've got left! Many can't cut loose from the past—past memories, past mistakes, past accomplishments, or past relationships.

Some can't forgive their past, so they brood, always feeling unworthy. They don't feel like they deserve to be happy or saved. Maybe they remember the stock-market crash and the Great Depression of the thirties and are afraid to invest, plan, and be creative!

The apostle Paul had a great attitude about life. He said, "Brothers, I do not consider myself yet to have taken hold of it. But one thing I do: Forgetting what is behind and straining toward what is ahead, I press on toward the goal to win the prize for which God has called me heavenward in Christ Jesus" (Phil. 3:13–14).

Suffering from the "Tomorrow Complex"

Although it's good to plan for the future, it's dangerous to live with a "tomorrow complex." Some people are always going to do it tomorrow. They don't realize that "someday" is not on the calendar and "someone" is not in the phone book. As my good friend, Zig Ziglar, would say, "We're either wandering generalities or meaningful specifics!" He carries little round, wooden coins with him that say "TUIT." He gives them to people who vow to do all sorts of good things when they "get around to it." Then comes his classic remark, "Now that you've got a *round tuit*, do it!"

Listen to this story of a famous procrastinator. While Paul was in prison, Governor Felix and his wife, Drusilla, visited him. One may wonder why they came to see Paul, considering their immoral reputation, but Paul seized the opportunity anyway. He preached to them of righteousness, temperance, and self-control. Scripture says Felix trembled. Then came his reply, "That's enough for now! You may leave. When I find it convenient, I will send for you" (Acts 24:25).

I once heard a fable about Satan and three of his imps. They were arguing about the best way to keep humans from becoming Christians. The first said, "I'll tell them there's no God!" The second said, "I'll tell them there's no hell!" The third said, "I'll tell them there's no hurry!" He got the job!

Many people live on the "someday" aisle. They say, "Someday I'll do this; someday I'll do that." But someday never comes.

Do It Now!

Remember that you've got today. Grab it with gusto. Use it with enthusiasm. Stay positive just for today. Fill each day with joy and gladness. Do good to others and think good thoughts. Most anyone can do this for one day. Then prop up that day with another one like it. You can have a positive and radiant life if you take things one day at a time.

Remember that you've got today. Grab it with gusto. Use it with enthusiasm.

Here are some powerful verses from the Bible on this way of life:

[Make] the most of every opportunity, because the days are evil! (Eph. 5:16)

As long as it is day, we must do the work of him who sent me. Night is coming, when no one can work. (John 9:4)

Choose for yourselves this day whom you will serve. . . . As for me and my household, we will serve the Lord. (Josh. 24:15)

Today if you will hear his voice, do not harden your hearts. (Heb. 4:7)

CHAPTER NINETEEN

But encourage one another daily, as long as it is called Today, so that none of you may be hardened by sin's deceitfulness. (Heb. 3:13)

Son, go and work today in the vineyard. (Matt. 21:28)

And now what are you waiting for? Get up, be baptized and wash away your sins, calling on his name. (Acts 22:16)

Now is the time of God's favor, now is the day of salvation. (2 Cor. 6:2)

Therefore do not worry about tomorrow, for tomorrow will worry about itself. Each day has enough trouble of its own. (Matt. 6:34)

Kay Lyons once said,

> Yesterday is a canceled check.
> Tomorrow is a promissory note.
> Today is the only cash you have.
> So spend it wisely!

Noted evangelist Charles Brown was preaching in the San Francisco Bay area for a packed house on Easter Sunday, 1906. "How differently I would have preached," he said later, "had I known many were hearing their last sermon before facing God." Before the next Sunday, the great San Francisco earthquake had hit, and thousands were killed.

I remember the conversion of Charley Tong, one of my friends from Australia. Charley was nearly eighty years old when he became a Christian. He had been a cinematographer in England during the days of silent motion pictures and had filmed many famous people, including Winston Churchill. He was inspired by a sign he saw on the wall of the home of one of England's great celebrities. It said "Do It Now!" That sign became the driving force behind many daring decisions he would make. When presented with the claims of Jesus, Charley's fears were completely swept aside with the philosophy that had dominated his life—do it now! He became a Christian with that same fervor with which he had lived his entire life. I'll never forget the night Charley died. He had a heart attack right in the middle of my Sunday night sermon and was dead before morning. But I'm sure his dying thoughts were that he was so glad he had stuck to his philosophy of "Do it now!"

So What Shall We Do with Today?

We need to grasp it, relish it, and thank God for it! But most of all, we should use it positively.

Don't miss God's opening and closing curtains—the sunrise and sunset! Tell someone you love them. Hug lots of people, lots of times. Make someone's day brighter. Laugh at things that are funny, because most things are! Draw nearer to God by talking to him, reading his Word, and recommitting your life to him. If you have just read this chapter, you must be alive, so TGI2DAY! Thank God it's today!

How to Make a Difference

She stood there in the aisle and said, "Excuse me." I got up to let her have the window seat. Two minutes later, another passenger came down the aisle, claiming the lady had his seat. To my seat-mate's surprise, she had the right plane and the right seat, but the wrong day! She was booked for the previous day. No matter, the flight attendant seated the gentleman in the seat in front of us, and the flight continued.

I say all this because I have learned that few things happen by accident. The lady told me it was no accident that we sat together. She said she needed the conversation we had on that flight. I got her address and sent her a copy of my last book. In reply, she sent me a starfish lapel pen with the following story:

A young boy, maybe ten, was alarmed at the number of starfish that had washed up on the beach. They would all be dead in a short time if not rescued. He was running along the beach, frantically throwing as many as he could back into the water. An amused man who had been watching called out to the boy: "Boy, there must be a million of these things on the beach. How do you figure you're going to make a difference?" The boy picked up another starfish and flung him back into the sea. "Made a difference for that one!" he said.

The note from my sweet seatmate added, "I have a feeling you make a difference wherever you go!"

I was highly complimented. It's a marvelous little story, but more than that, it's a wonderful philosophy of life.

Surrounded by Starfish

We are faced with many problems on this earth that we'll never solve, like those millions of starfish on the shore. We'll never make a dent in them. We read about an earthquake in India that takes thousands of lives. We care, but what can we do? We can't solve the situation, so we move on to the comics and the sports page. Malnutrition and starvation steals countless numbers of lives in Bosnia and Croatia. Thousands of people in South Africa suffer from poverty. It is beyond description, even though I've been there and have seen it with my own eyes. In the newspapers, we read about Saddam Hussein slaying unbelievable numbers of his political enemies in Iraq. What can we do? There's no way one person can negotiate peace between the Israelis and the Arabs or between the Catholics and Protestants in Ireland.

On the home front, it doesn't get much better. It seems like the number of teenage pregnancies escalates every year. More children are having children. How can I help? How can one person fix all the scandals from Watergate to Whitewater? How can I stop the corruption that regularly goes on among politicians?

Every year, the number of people dying from AIDS increases. There are so many hurts, so much poverty and turmoil, and so many in tragic circumstances. It staggers the imagination. What can one person do? How can we make a difference?

The Little Boy Had the Right Idea

I'm thankful the young boy didn't just throw up his hands and give up. He just couldn't walk away. He knew more starfish would die than would be rescued by his feeble efforts. He felt his limitations, but he cared enough to make a difference—if only for one!

What's the significance of one, you might ask? Jesus explained it with three stories in Luke 15. First, he told of a shepherd who was concerned about one little, lost sheep. The shepherd left the other ninety-nine sheep in the fold and searched all night for one lost lamb. Then he told of a woman who lit a candle and swept the whole house to find one missing coin. Finally, he told of a father, who watched the horizon every day in hopes that his runaway son would return. And when he did, the father ran to the boy, embraced him, and kissed him. He ordered a feast and invited all his neighbors to a banquet for his son. In the same way, the Bible says, "There will be more rejoicing in heaven over one sinner that repents than over ninety-

He felt his limitations, but he cared enough to make a difference —if only for one!

nine righteous persons who do not need to repent" (Luke 15:7).

I saw a marvelous demonstration a few years back at a Promise Keepers rally in Colorado. They called for lights out in the stadium, and one man lit a candle. He touched it to the candle of the person on his right and on his left. Each of them began to light the candles next to them. In a short time, the stadium radiated with the light of fifty thousand candles. In the same way, when one person makes a difference in the life of another, it has a phenomenal effect.

You Can Make a Difference for One

As writer Edward Everett Hale once said, "I am only one, but still I am one." All of us have eyes to see what's going on around us. We have ears to hear of the tragic plight of so many. It's true we don't have enough money to pay off all the debts or enough energy to reach out to all the hurting. But we have *some* money, *some* time, and *some* gifts that will help us make a difference in the life of someone who needs us.

America is experiencing a great breakdown in its homes. More than a million times last year, a gavel came down in a courtroom, and a judge pronounced the words, "Divorce granted!" You can't solve all the marriage problems in the world, but you can resolve to love your own husband or wife. There are lots of troubled kids out there, and you may never be able to help each one, but you can reach out to one. You can spend quality time with your own son or daughter. Give them your personal time, personal love, and personal discipline. You can commit them individually to the Lord.

We used to have a singing group at church called the "Heaven Generation Singers." There was a resolution behind the name. Each member had to promise to commit his life to Christ. They vowed to marry only a Christian and raise each of their children to love and serve Jesus. By following this pact, they would be able to raise a generation of people on their way to heaven.

The church should be an oasis in the desert, yet many are only mirages. Some are more interested in the building than the people. You can't change all churches, but you can make a difference in your own church. Get behind your minister and give him your time and talents. You can make your church a brighter place, radiating with the love of Jesus. Others will notice and glorify God!

Then there are all the poor, sick, and down-and-out. There are so many. We can't help them all. We don't have the resources, time, or opportunities. But as the Bible says, "As we have opportunity, let us do good to all people, especially to those who belong to the family of believers" (Gal. 6:10).

Before I left on my last trip to South Africa, a children's foundation gave me fifteen hundred dollars to spend on the kids there. We probably didn't make a dent in the total poverty of the nation, but we helped a lot of people. What fun it is to be involved in something so worthwhile. I understand the joy of the little boy who tried to save the starfish.

What about evangelism? So many are lost and have never heard about Jesus. So many who have heard have never committed their lives to him. Jesus told us, "Go into all the world and preach the good news to all creation" (Mark 16:15). Many more don't know Jesus than do, so each person can win at least one for Christ. That's what insurance men call EMGAM (Every Man Get a Man).

In the hospital one day, I looked into the eyes of a man I had recently led to Christ. In earlier days, he had been an alcoholic. It had cost him his health, his job, his wife, and soon, his life. Fortunately, I had been able to share the sweet story of Jesus with him. He had responded in repentance and was baptized. He was now saved and right with God. I'll never forget the look on his face or the tears in his eyes as he looked at me and said, "You saved my soul!" See, we made a difference to this one!

This is the best way to live. It's the most rewarding and the most satisfying course to follow. It is pure fun to make a difference for even one!

Start Making a Difference in Your Own Life

You really can't change anyone but yourself! You read about all the alcoholics, adulterers, unwed mothers, unfit fathers, thieves, liars, gossips, juvenile delinquents, and troublemakers in the world. They live in your neighborhood, work in your office, and may even attend your church. But you don't have to be any of these! You have the power of choice. You can decide to live a life of integrity. You can keep your promises, shoulder your responsibility, do your own duty, and serve the Lord Jesus Christ.

You can decide to become a Christian whether anyone else does or not. You can serve in Christ's blood-bought church even if everyone else takes another route. No force on earth or in hell can keep you from living right and going to heaven when you die.

Let Christ Make a Difference in Your Life!

What a difference Jesus can make in each and every life. He forgave his murderers and made them the first members of his church (see Acts 2:37–47). He turned a persecutor into a preacher (see Acts 9). He cleaned up homosexuals, male prostitutes, drunkards, and swindlers and adopted them all into his family (see 1 Cor. 6:9–11). He can make a difference in your life if you just let him, but he won't renovate a house he doesn't own.

Jesus says, "Here I am! I stand at the door and knock. If anyone hears my voice and opens the door, I will come in and eat with him, and he with me" (Rev. 3:20).

A young artist handed his picture to his teacher. The teacher said, "Your picture is not finished. There's no knob on your door!" The artist responded, "That's the door to the human heart. There's no knob on the outside of the door. It must be opened from the inside!"

Jesus is knocking at your door! Let him in! It will make all the difference in the world!

He Profits Most
Who Serves Best

"He profits most who serves best!" This is the Rotary International motto and the philosophy of multibillionaire Ted Turner.

Turner, founder of Turner Broadcasting Service and CNN, was speaking in Oklahoma City for the annual Oklahoma Business Conference. During the conference, Turner told the audience, "Generous people are happier than stingy old misers."

Turner must know what he's talking about because a couple of years ago, he made international news over his plans to give the United Nations a gift of one billion dollars. Now, he's urging other billionaires to do the same.

Although not too many of my readers are billionaires, most of you will agree that Turner's philosophy is economically sound, psychologically solid, and biblically correct. And someone a lot more famous than Ted Turner said it a long time ago. Jesus said, "It is more blessed to give than to receive" (Acts 20:35).

Serving with a Smile

In the article, Turner was quoted as saying, "You don't get honor from making money. You're honored for giving money!" He claimed that the more generous you are, the more fun you have. He also added that you don't need money in heaven, and it sure won't do you any good in hell!

Turner urged his audience to laugh more and develop a positive mental attitude by cultivating a sense of humor. Turner said that one of his achievements is his cartoon network, which has ratings four times higher than CNN's. People enjoy watching Bugs Bunny, Tom and Jerry, and Wile E. Coyote because, as Turner says, "They're a gas!" He also prided himself on his positive, upbeat attitude and said that people don't like to be around miserable, depressed people. The article quotes him as saying, "I've never seen anyone be happy when money was their god!"

Turner credits three things with helping him succeed—a curious mind, an interest in different businesses, and a desire to help his customers. As an active Rotarian, he cites the Rotary motto, "He profits most who serves best!"

Does This Philosophy Really Work?

Is this something the average man can sink his teeth into, or is it simply the idle ramblings of a guy who happens to be filthy rich? You see, this isn't about money at all. This idea applies just as much to the laborer as it does to the billionaire. It's a lifestyle choice. It's an attitude about serving rather than demanding to be served.

Years ago Garson L. Rice of Greensboro, North Carolina, set the world's record in Toyota sales, selling 904 cars in a single month. The *Arkansas Gazette* carried his story. While he didn't offer a formula for success, he emphasized seven principles that he used to run his business.

1. Persistence
2. Expectation
3. Concentration
4. Excellence
5. Enthusiasm
6. Advertising
7. People

Rice said, "We're not in the automobile business at all. We're in the *people business,* helping others solve their transportation problems. When you give good products and services to others, you insure your own success and happiness." Every success story in American industry has followed the same creed.

Giving is the key to success in every endeavor of life! It is true in marriage, parenting, and friendships. It's also true in one's spiritual life.

Jesus Modeled Sacrificial Giving

Jesus was the greatest teacher who ever lived. Once the apostles were having a little "Muhammad Ali" contest (you know, "I'm the greatest!"). As Jesus walked up to them, they quieted down. They didn't want him to know they were vying for the top position in heaven. Jesus gave them some real advice about how to "climb the ladder." He said, "Whoever wants to become great among you must be your servant" (Matt. 20:26).

Ted Turner's one-billion-dollar gift is great, but it pales in comparison to the gift Jesus gave this world. For "the gift of God is eternal life in Christ Jesus our Lord" (Rom. 6:23).

Life Is about Giving

Jesus taught, "Give, and it will be given to you. A good measure, pressed down, shaken together and running over, will be poured into your lap. For with the measure you use, it will be measured to you" (Luke 6:38).

Giving isn't about sending money to some TV ministry; it's about helping others, giving time, and sharing. It's about reaching out and showing compassion and understanding. It's about loving, forgiving, and going the second mile!

Life isn't about how much you can accumulate; it's about how you use what you've got! You can't take it with you. When billionaire H. L. Hunt died, someone asked, "I wonder how much money old man Hunt left?" The answer was simple, "He left it all!"

Life isn't about how much you can accumulate; it's about how you use what you've got!

Many will remember the story of Jim Elliott and four friends who were killed back in the fifties in an Ecuadorian jungle while trying to preach the gospel to the Auca Indians. Many books have been written about their adventures. When Jim was nineteen, he wrote in his journal, "He is no fool who gives what he cannot keep to gain what he cannot lose!" Jim was twenty-five when he lost his life. But he gained eternal life through the sacrifice of a terminal life that he couldn't have kept for long anyway!

It Pays to Serve Jesus

The most important gift you can give to Jesus is your life. It pays the most and brings the most rewards.

I was rummaging through some old cassette tapes in my office. I ran across the last one I received from my aged mother before she died of a heart attack at age eighty. Mom was a country woman, and "new fangled gadgets" were hard for her. She thought she had to completely fill up that tape, so as she ran out of things to tell me, she began to sing this beautiful song by Frank C. Huston:

> The service of Jesus true pleasure affords;
> In Him there is joy without an alloy;
> 'Tis heaven to trust Him and rest on His words;
> It pays to serve Jesus each day.

The tape ran out as she began the chorus. These were the last recorded words of my mother. "It pays to serve Jesus, it pays . . ."

And dear friends, it does!

Friends in High Places

Garth Brooks was in Tulsa recently, entertaining his fellow Oklahomans with his chart-topping country songs and his magnificent stage presence. He sang them all, eventually getting around to the old, crowd-pleasing favorite, "Friends in Low Places."

Everybody needs friends. In Jess Lair's great little book, *I Ain't Much, Baby, but I'm All I Got,* he says everyone needs at least five good friends, the kind of friends who would give you the shirts off their backs. The kind that will always be there for you, no matter how low the places are that you find yourself in. Someone else said we need a minimum of seven such friends. "You're going to need them when you die," he said. "Six to carry and one to preach!"

About the worst thing that can happen to anyone is to be alone and lonely. Or in a crowd and lonely. A person who has good friends is rich indeed.

The Wrong Kind of Friends

Friends are valuable to us, but they need to be the right kind of friends. As Garth Brooks sang, some of our friends may come from low places. The Bible tells a story about Amnon having another kind of friend (see 2 Sam. 13:3). Amnon fell in love with his stepsister Tamar, literally aching to have her. Amnon confided his lust to Jonadab, who was the wrong kind of friend. He suggested an evil scheme to Amnon.

Following Jonadab's plan, Amnon pretended he was ill and sent for Tamar, asking her to come to his room and prepare some food for him. She innocently agreed. But once he had her in his room with the door locked behind her, Amnon raped her. Amnon's friend had given him terrible advice, leading him to commit a crime causing shame and hatred for both Amnon and his stepsister. The situation eventually led to Amnon's murder.

Friends can be valuable resources, but the wrong kind of friends can be dangerous. As Paul warned the Corinthians, "Do not be misled: 'Bad company corrupts good character'" (1 Cor. 15:33).

David and Jonathan

One of the Bible's best stories about friendship describes the enduring relationship between David and Jonathan (see 1 and 2 Sam.). It wasn't easy for the two young men to be friends, because Jonathan was King Saul's son, and Saul, fearful that David would succeed him as king, was continually trying to kill David. Nevertheless, the friendship endured.

When Jonathan interceded with King Saul on David's behalf, it nearly cost Jonathan his own life. But whenever David needed to "find strength in God," he turned to Jonathan, who was always there to help him. The Bible says, "Jonathan loved David as himself," and David described their friendship as "more wonderful than the love of women." Such a friendship is a rare and beautiful gift.

The Bible speaks highly of the right kind of friends. Proverbs 17:17 says, "A friend loves at all times." And Ecclesiastes 4:9–12 reminds us: "Two are better than one. . . . If one falls down, his friend can help him up. But pity the man who falls and has no one to help him up! Also, if two lie down together, they will keep warm. But how can one keep warm alone? Though one may be overpowered, two can defend themselves. A cord of three strands is not quickly broken."

Friends in High Places

Jehovah God, Creator of the universe and the heavenly Father, wants to be your friend. This fact may be the greatest thing you can know in life. God wants to be your friend just as he was a friend to Moses and Abraham. Exodus 33:11 says, "The Lord would speak to Moses face to face, as a man speaks with his friend." James 2:23 says, "Abraham believed God, and it was credited to him as righteousness," and he was called God's friend.

God, your Friend in high places, will always love you. He will always be there for you.

So I say to you: Ask and it will be given to you; seek and you will find; knock and the door will be opened to you. For everyone who asks receives; he who seeks finds; and to him who knocks, the door will be opened.

Which of you fathers, if your son asks for a fish, will give him a snake instead? Or if he asks for an egg, will give him a scorpion? If you then, though you are evil, know how to give good gifts to your children, how much more will your Father in heaven give the Holy Spirit to those who ask him! (Luke 11:9–13)

God's Son, Jesus Christ, wants to be your friend too. He was called "a friend of . . . sinners" (Luke 7:34). It was said in derision, but it was a phrase Jesus liked.

As the words of that grand old song by Joseph M. Scriven proclaim:

> What a friend we have in Jesus,
> All our sins and griefs to bear;
> What a privilege to carry
> Everything to God in prayer.

Solomon said, "There is a friend who sticks closer than a brother" (Prov. 18:24). That friend is Jesus!

The Holy Spirit is also our friend, our "Comforter." Scripture says he lives in all of God's children. He will lead and guide our lives if we let him. So without a doubt, we can claim him as another one of our marvelous "friends in high places."

Angel Friends

We also have angel friends, "thousands upon thousands of angels in joyful assembly" (Heb. 12:22). Here's a little glimpse of what the Bible tells us about these celestial beings:

> He will command his angels concerning you to guard you in all your ways. (Ps. 91:11)

See that you do not look down on one of these little ones. For I tell you that their angels in heaven always see the face of my Father in heaven. (Matt. 18:10)

Angels carried [Lazarus] to Abraham's side. (Luke 16:22)

Are not all angels ministering spirits sent to serve those who will inherit salvation? (Heb. 1:14)

Do not forget to entertain strangers, for by so doing some people have entertained angels without knowing it. (Heb. 13:2)

Friends in the Heavenly Grandstand

Hebrews 11 has been called Faith's Hall of Fame. It mentions great Bible characters such as Enoch, Noah, Abraham, Isaac, Jacob, Joseph, Moses, and many others. I like to think of these Bible heroes filling the heavenly grandstand, watching our efforts here on earth, and cheering us on to victory. And there, sitting beside them in those high-altitude bleachers, are our loved ones who died as Christians. They, too, cheer us on as we limp along through this earthly life.

When we feel burdened beyond belief, when we want to give up, doesn't it feel great to know our friends are up there in the grandstand, watching us, believing in us, cheering us on? What a comfort it is to know we have such heavenly friends, that they want us to make it. They see our burdens. They know how it feels. And they also know we can make it, just as they made it.

I've preached many funerals, and I know without a doubt that up in heaven there are fathers and mothers, husbands and wives, cheering us on. There are young children there, too, rooting for us. Knowing they are there makes heaven seem even sweeter. Surely we cannot fail knowing we've got such friends in high places!

Friends in the Family of God

Many times in the Bible, Christians are referred to as friends. Many of the epistles include a salutation to friends. Third John concludes with the note, "I hope to see you soon, and we will talk face to face. Peace to you. The friends here send their greetings. Greet the friends there by name" (v. 14).

God's people really are friends. As I travel all across the United States and in Australia and South Africa, visiting with fellow Christians, I am treated warmly as a friend wherever I go. I am treated as dear family.

Cleon Lyles once said, "Every preacher is someone's big preacher!" George Bailey is mine. He came to Australia back in the sixties when my family was there. His invaluable ministry and encouragement have continued through the years. I have traveled with him to the Bible Lands three times, and on each trip his personal encouragement has helped me immeasurably. On my sixty-sixth birthday, he called just to express his love and friendship. What a blessing to have such a friend!

I'll never forget my 1996 trip to South Africa. I was facing retirement and knew this would probably be my last time to go. I would no longer have a church to send me there as the Garnett church had done since 1986. While I was in that rather bittersweet emotional state, native South African evangelist Peter Ford befriended me. We talked in depth, and we prayed together. He assured me that the Lord would find a way, and his supportive friendship meant more to me than he could have known.

And he was right. In June 1997, a ninety-two-year-old viewer of my TV program died and left me a trust fund providing the means to go to South Africa for the next five years. Friendship and the providence of God—aren't they wonderful?

When I had cancer surgery in April 1995, friends from all over the world wrote encouragingly to say they were praying for me. Their support was surely a factor in my steady recovery.

> Friendship and the providence of God— aren't they wonderful?

We are never strangers when we travel among Christians. We may speak different languages. Our customs and cultures may be vastly different. But when we are among Christians we are among friends—marvelous members of God's family, both here on earth and in the highest places!

Oasis in the Desert

It was hot and dry in the desert of Beersheba. Hagar tilted the water skin to her mouth and took a sip. Then she handed it to her son. "Drink the rest," she said.

Together they squinted in the blazing noonday sun. They both knew what was going to happen. Vultures began circling overhead.

They had had a few happy years. It had all started when God promised Abraham and Sarah a son. One who would be the necessary link to God's three promises to Abraham—to make him into a great nation, to give him a land in which to live, and to bless all families of the earth through his seed.

Abraham and Sarah were both beyond childbearing years when the promise was given. They waited more than ten years but had no son. They began to become impatient, so Sarah suggested that Abraham take her handmaid, Hagar, and sire a child by her. Their motives were pure, but their faith, at that point, was weak!

Abraham was one hundred years old when Isaac was finally born to the ninety-year-old Sarah. He was the child of God's promise. As Issac grew, Sarah's resentment and jealousy toward Hagar increased. At Sarah's insistence, Hagar and Ishmael were banished. Abraham sadly gave them a little food and water and pointed them toward the desert. It was dry and hot, and there wasn't a chance they would survive.

Hagar couldn't bear to watch her young son die. She helped him into the shade of a small bush and went off a distance to pray and to cry. God heard their cries and sent an angel to tell them not to be afraid. The angel promised that Ishmael would live. Then he showed them a well of water—an oasis right in the middle of the desert.

Have You Ever Been in a Desert?

Maybe you've actually been in a desert. At least you've seen them in movies. You've watched men stagger along the dusty land with dry skin and parched throats, carrying empty canteens. Buzzards, waiting patiently for their next meal, circle around them.

Suddenly, they shout excitedly as they see lovely palm trees circling a pool of sparkling, silver blue water. They run toward it and fall into the sand. But it's only a mirage.

It's so refreshing to see an oasis right in the middle of the desert. There's a big difference between a mirage and an oasis. One is life-defeating, while the other is life-giving.

When I rode through the Nullabor Plain in Australia on a narrow gauge train, I complained about the discomfort of the train. But if I had been walking through the desert instead of sitting inside the train, I would not have survived. Someone said you could take a picture out the window every hour all day long, and it would be the same picture. A lone pub would dot the desert about every two hundred miles. I've also been on the road between Jerusalem and Gaza. It's a desert. It doesn't have the usual sand dunes, just miles of deserted area. Jericho was its oasis. After traveling through that desert, it's so refreshing to come into Jericho with its locust trees and fruit stands. Orange juice never tasted better!

Our World Is a Desert

Our world is a desert—and people know it. They don't necessarily know that they are lost from God and facing judgment unprepared, but they sense that our world is a barren and lonely place. The media daily describes, with distinct accuracy, the desert we live in. Bible warnings of the last days read like the front page of the *New York Times* or the *Washington Post.*

> But mark this: There will be terrible times in the last days. People will be lovers of themselves, lovers of money, boastful, proud, abusive, disobedient to their parents, ungrateful, unholy, without love, unforgiving, slanderous, without self-control, brutal, not lovers of the good, treacherous, rash, conceited, lovers of pleasure rather than lovers of God—having a form of godliness but denying its power. (2 Tim. 3:1–5)

Many Third-World countries are plagued with famine, war, starvation, atrocities, and hopelessness. Even in America, we don't know where to turn. Many are without jobs, proper food, or clothing. Many are friendless, homeless, helpless, and hopeless. People of our nation, and those abroad, know we're living in a desert.

Everyone Is Looking for an Oasis!

Hurting people are seeking an oasis—a place where peace reigns and problems don't exist, a utopia, if you will. The difference between those who have found the oasis and those who haven't is knowing where to look.

Psychiatrists' couches are full because people aren't living the way they were designed to live. We were designed to spend our days seeking our Master and Designer.

Specialists try to help people find their oases. Self-help books, tapes, and seminars abound. "Get-rich-quick" schemes are all over the place. But still the oasis eludes us. People turn to noise, danger, miracle drugs, and elixirs in their search for an oasis. People with terminal diseases run to Mexico and Greece and take anything from ginseng to apricot pits in search of cures.

Most of us have our oasis fairly well defined. Just ask someone, "What will it take to make you happy?" The answer usually involves a certain amount of money. "I want enough to pay all my bills, pay off my house, buy myself a new car, and go to Hawaii, Acapulco, or Paris!" A few people may describe their oasis as having a good marriage and family. Yet almost none talks about finding it in a personal, solid relationship with God!

Running to Mirages in the Desert

There's nothing inherently wrong with money. Like the old saying goes, "Money won't buy happiness, but it will help you to be miserable in a better part of town!" We should have learned from the lives of a few rich failures that the oasis can't be bought with money! Like Ecclesiastes 5:10 says, "Whoever loves money never has money enough; whoever loves wealth is never satisfied with his income."

The oasis can't be achieved with more toys. Americans own a lot of toys. Our list of necessities is considerably longer than it was a generation ago. We want bigger and better homes and cars. We claim that we need lake homes and ski boats. We want sporting equipment and trips to exotic places.

The oasis can't be found in illicit sex. One-night stands do not lead to lasting or satisfying long-term relationships. James Bond-type romances do not bring us peace of mind or a healthy self-esteem. Instead, they cause unwanted pregnancies, sexually transmitted diseases, and AIDS!

The oasis can't be found in more power, more travel, more thrills, or more danger. We are looking for it in all the wrong places. As the Bible says, "There is a way that seems right to a man, but in the end it leads to death" (Prov. 14:12).

Where Is the Oasis?

Finding the oasis is an inside job. Achieving inner peace involves making good decisions and setting the right priorities. It comes from building lasting, genuine, and healthy relationships. You're only as rich as your relationships. It doesn't stem from loving things and using people, but from loving people and using things! It comes from making genuine, permanent commitments in marriage and forming lasting, unconditional relationships with your kids, your loved ones, and your friends.

> Finding the oasis is an inside job.

Most of all, the oasis has a name and its name is Jesus! He's the answer to all of life's unanswerable questions.

> Submit to God and be at peace with him; in this way prosperity will come to you. (Job 22:21)

> The thief comes only to steal and kill and destroy; I have come that they may have life, and have it to the full. (John 10:10)

> I am the way and the truth and the life. (John 14:6)

> Apart from me you can do nothing. (John 15:5)

> For to me, to live is Christ; and to die is gain. (Phil. 1:21)

It's not so bad to live in the desert if you know where the oasis is. And it can be found in Jesus. If you're searching for him, that's good, but you should know he's been searching for you a lot longer than you've been searching for him. The oasis has a vacancy, so reserve your room today!

I Choose to Believe

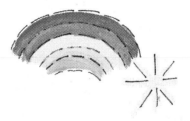

Most of the world's population can be divided into pairs of opposites: men and women, tall and short, fat and skinny, rich and poor, educated and uneducated, positive and negative thinkers, happy and sad, hungry and full, healthy and sick, free and enslaved, dead and alive. The possibilities are endless. But the greatest difference occurs—now and throughout eternity—between believers and unbelievers.

An Age of Doubters

Many people doubt God. Some may believe he exists but doubt that he cares. Many doubt the Bible and the church, pointing to the many scandals and acts of chicanery among religious leaders. They doubt the motives of philanthropists and question the motives of those claiming to be moral, generous, benevolent, and forgiving. They cast a suspicious eye toward those who do good and question the faith of churchgoers.

Missouri is known as the "Show Me State" because its citizens are said to be skeptical about anything until they've seen it with their own eyes. This "seeing is believing" attitude may be to blame for the doubt that's troubling many in our world today. People say they search for God and fail to find him. But people who doubt that God exists are not looking in the right direction!

When John Glenn became the first American to circle the earth, his Russian counterparts, who discounted any belief in God, asked him, "Did you see God while you were up there?"

John Glenn replied with a twinkle in his eye, "No, I didn't see him, but I'm confident he saw me!"

Faith to See through the Storm!

God is there, all right. But at times it is admittedly difficult to see him. It's easy to doubt that God exists when bad things happen to good people. It's hard to see God's involvement in our lives when the doctor has just hit us with the word *terminal* in describing our own or a loved one's condition. When things are at their worst, it is hard to see God at his best.

The apostle Paul had what he called a thorn in the flesh (see 2 Cor. 12:7–10). We are not told exactly what it was, probably so we can relate it to our own various "thorns." Many scholars believe Paul's "thorn" was a horrible eye disease, a terrible affliction that caused ugly, painful secretions. If true, the condition made Paul difficult to look at, much less listen to. Perhaps knowing that his appearance was so repugnant that people failed to hear his message, Paul begged God to heal him. He *knew* God could do it; he had seen him heal others. In fact, God had worked such miracles through Paul himself. And most importantly, Paul would use the healing to God's glory.

But for some reason God refused. "My grace is sufficient for you," God told the weary evangelist.

Paul accepted God's decision. You see, he believed in the Healer, not the healing, so he was able to trust God and move on. Oh, how you and I need that kind of belief today!

God is there, all right. He sees and cares. But his timetable is better than ours. Someday we'll be able to understand how his schedule was perfect, while ours was flawed. Someday we will know the reason behind his every yes, no, or not now.

Living by Faith

On a recent trip to Australia, I flew on a magnificent 747 jetliner, an awesome airplane that has more than three million parts. As the huge machine climbed skyward, I looked around and thought about the complicated assembly of computer chips, hydraulic lines, electrical systems, and instrument panels—put together by the lowest bidder. And hadn't I just read somewhere that this airline's maintenance crew had gone on strike not long ago, complaining about poor treatment from the company? The plane was flown by a crew I did not know. Had they been drinking before we took off? Had they gotten plenty of rest the night before? The opportunities to worry were plentiful. Yet there I was, enjoying the flight, sleeping peacefully through the night. It was a flight of faith, faith in the company that had built the plane and faith in the airline's maintenance crew, cockpit crew, and flight attendants.

At the other end of the airline spectrum, I recently flew on a small commuter plane between St. Louis and Cape Girardeau, Missouri; there were about six of us aboard. You could see the pilot and copilot at work in the cockpit, busily doing the preflight check from the standard manual, verifying that everything was ready for takeoff. The lady across the narrow aisle from me had never been on such a small plane before. She leaned over to me with a worried look on her face and asked, "What's that book they're looking at?"

I said, "Well, the name of it is *How to Fly an Airplane.*"

She was not impressed with my humor.

Another guy quipped, "I hate it when the pilot comes through the cabin asking if any of us has jumper cables!"

Yes, I fly regularly, and no matter what size the airplane is, I usually sleep like a baby as we soar across the skies. This is faith; it's also the way we all live whether we fly or drive or walk. As tourists we drive through areas we've never been in before, stop at a gas station we've never traded with, and confidently pump that station's gasoline into our tanks, believing it's a good product that will make our cars go without causing damage. We walk on sidewalks beside busy, traffic-filled streets, believing the drivers will stay on the pavement and not swerve over to our strip of concrete. We do these things every day because we have faith in our fellow human beings. Yet some people say, "I have no faith in God; there's no evidence that he exists. It makes no sense to believe."

Arrival or Survival?

Is our world an accident, or did it happen on purpose? Well, consider this question: Most of us wear wristwatches. If you have one, look at it and tell me: Did anyone make that watch? Or was it the evolution of the sun's rays striking a metal spring in a rubbish dump?

Does the watch prove the existence of a watchmaker? Or is it easier to believe that the watch was first a spring that evolved into a steam gauge and then, reacting to the sun, finally evolved into a timepiece complete with case, band, and rotating hands? Creation proves a creator. Design proves a designer. Humans were created and designed by the living God.

The theory of evolution makes about as much sense as the story about the man who went hunting in Africa. He spotted a big lioness and raised his gun to fire, but the gun jammed. The lioness chased him into an old pickle factory where the man spotted a barrel and promptly pulled it down over himself. The lion jumped up onto the top of the barrel. When the hunter peeped out through the bunghole on the side of the barrel, he could see the lioness's tail swishing back and forth. In desperation he reached out and grabbed the tail, tying it into a knot inside the barrel. When the lioness jumped down, she took the barrel with her. The hunter watched in amazement as the lioness bounded off over the hill with her tail knotted inside that barrel.

The next year he was hunting in the same area and claims he saw that same lioness again. The barrel was still bouncing around behind her with her tail knotted inside, he said. Not only that, but she had two little cubs with her, and each cub had the end of its little tail knotted inside a barrel too!

That kind of "evolution" makes about as much sense as the idea that man has descended from a fish to a monkey to a human. Here's another evolutionary tale to make you chuckle:

> Three monkeys sat in a coconut tree,
> Discussing things as they are said to be.

CHAPTER TWENTY-FOUR

Said one to the others, "Now, listen, you two,

There's a rumor around that can't be true,

That man descended from our noble race;

The very idea is a great disgrace!

No monkey has ever deserted his wife,

Starved her babies and ruined her life.

And you've never known a mother monk

To leave her babies with others to bunk,

Or pass from one on to another

Till they scarcely know who is their mother.

Here's another thing a monkey won't do:

Go out at night and get on a stew,

Or use a gun or club or knife

To take some other monkey's life!

Yes, man descended, the ornery cuss,

But brothers, he didn't descend from us!"

Is It Really Incredible to Believe in God?

The Bible defines faith as "the substance of things hoped for, the evidence of things not seen" (Heb. 11:1 KJV). There's more evidence that God exists than there is that Abraham Lincoln or George Washington ever lived.

And there's just as much evidence that the Bible is the Word of God. Consider the library of sixty-six books in the Bible, thirty-nine in the Old Testament and twenty-seven in the New. The Bible was written over a period of about sixteen hundred years with more than forty different people having a part in its writing. Yet it contains no contradictions historically, geographically, or geologically. The Bible is not a history book, and it isn't a book on geography or geology either. It is the Word of an almighty God, and that means it must be 100 percent accurate in all categories. That's what makes the following statements phenomenal when you consider that at the time they were written, people did not generally believe these facts:

- Air has weight (see Job 28:25).
- The earth is round (see Isa. 40:22).
- There is a hole in the northern sky (see Job 26:7).

In the forties when archaeologists discovered the Dead Sea Scrolls, people wondered what changes these older and more accurate translations would cause in our modern Bibles. And then what changes would we have to make in our belief system as a result of those biblical changes? Instead, the Dead Sea Scrolls confirmed that we have an accurate translation of the Bible in our hands today.

> There's more evidence that God exists than there is that Abraham Lincoln or George Washington ever lived.

Archaeologists continue to learn more about early civilization, but as someone said, "Every time an archaeologist turns over a spade, it authenticates the Bible all over again."

This truth was illustrated for me during a trip to the Bible Lands, when my tour group was traveling through ancient Corinth. Discussing how those who oppose the Bible argue the existence of the character Erastus (mentioned in Rom. 16:23), our guide showed us a fallen doorway, clearly visible near an amphitheater as yet unearthed. When the amphitheater is completely uncovered, the doorway will stand erect and all will be able to view its inscription:

ERASTUS, DIRECTOR OF PUBLIC WORKS.

Believing in the Bible makes more sense than doubting it!

Some Logical Conclusions

Creation proves we have a Creator. His existence is no harder to believe than the existence of a toymaker, watchmaker, or house-builder. Yet we have a choice. We can choose to believe that God exists and that the Bible is a revelation from God and of God, our handbook on how our Creator wants us to live. Or we can choose to disbelieve. Either way, we're going to give an account to our Creator someday for what we have done with the life he has given us. All parables of Jesus point to the fact that one day he will return for this reckoning. Our decision to believe or disbelieve this fact will affect the quality of our lives now—and a million years from now.

As for myself, I choose to believe that God exists and that the Bible is his Word. I believe it without a shred of doubt. What do you choose to believe?

25

We'll Leave the Light On

He sat in my office wringing his hands. He was a father of six, and his oldest daughter was giving him trouble, again! She was threatening to leave home. He told her that if she did, she could never come back. He asked me if he had said the right thing to her. Well, there was merit to his statement. If you make your own bed, you'll have to sleep in it. And the Bible does say, "A man reaps what he sows" (Gal. 6:7). But if the prodigal son's father had said that, the fifteenth chapter of Luke would not be in the Bible.

The Runaway

In Luke 15, the crowd simply didn't understand the fatherly nature of God, so Jesus told them a story. A certain father had two sons. The youngest was tired of all the rules. He wanted all the perks in life but wasn't willing to work for them. So he made an announcement to his father. "Hey, old man," he said, "I'm tired of all these rules. I want a life of my own. I'm going someplace where I can be free. They tell me the grass is greener out there. People do as they please and have fun. I'm breaking out of here. Just give me what's coming to me first." So the boy left home with high hopes and bulging pockets, containing his part of the family inheritance.

He lived the high life for a while. His pockets were always full, and the drinks were on him! He had plenty of friends, as long as he was picking up the tab. But soon the money ran out. We don't know how he spent his money, but the Bible says he "squandered his wealth in wild living" (v. 13). His older brother accused him of blowing it on prostitutes—maybe because that's what he would have done if he had been in the far country. I don't think we were meant to know what Jesus meant by "wild living," because he wanted us to insert our own sins for that part of the story!

A famine came, and soon the money was gone. A famine always seems to come to those who turn their backs on God and go their own way. The boy got hungry and needed a job. Nobody would give him anything. Then one day, there it was in the classifieds:

WANTED: Stupid boy to slop pigs!

He qualified! He was so desperate that he took the job. He was even tempted to eat the slop he poured out for the hogs. He had hit rock bottom.

The Rest of the Story

Alcoholics Anonymous has helped thousands who suffer from alcoholism, but they say a person has to hit bottom before he or she can be helped. The boy in the pigpen was at the bottom and was ripe for either salvation or suicide. I shudder to think about how many have chosen suicide. Fortunately, the pigpen became the boy's salvation. He woke up and saw things as they really were. He said to himself, "Back at home even the servants do better than me." He thought about going home but doubted he'd be accepted back. He knew he didn't deserve a second chance. It was his own fault that he had fallen.

Yet, even though he didn't know *where* to turn, he knew to *whom* to turn!

"I'm going home to my father," he said. And he did. What a surprise he got when he found his father waiting for him. The father saw him coming while he was still a long way off. He'd been out there every day, scanning the horizon, hoping to catch a glimpse of his son. And today it happened. He saw the boy and was filled with compassion. He broke into a dead run, and when he reached his son he "threw his arms around him and kissed him" (v. 20). Then he directed his servants to bring the VIP robe, new shoes, and a ring for his son's hand. He ordered the cooks to kill the calf they'd been fattening up in anticipation of this very day. Then he threw a party in his son's honor. There was music and dancing; it was the party of all parties. And then he tells us this good news: "I tell you that in the same way there will be more rejoicing in heaven over one sinner who repents than over ninety-nine righteous persons who do not need to repent" (v. 7).

All Stories Don't End That Way

Their son was in Vietnam, and they were very concerned about him. He was in the infantry and in the thick of battle. They hadn't heard from him in a long time. Then one day he called from California.

The war was over for him, and he was on his way home! He explained that he had a buddy with him, who had been wounded pretty badly. His friend only had one arm, one leg, and one eye, and no other place to go. "Can I bring my friend home with me?" he asked. His parents explained that, of course, he could bring his buddy home for a while, but that they couldn't be expected to take care of him for long.

Later, they received a telegram from Washington D.C., explaining that their son had committed suicide in California by jumping from a twelve-story building. Imagine how shocked they were when they came to claim his body and saw that he only had one arm, one leg, and one eye!

We All Need to Know the Light Is On!

Tom Bodette does that clever commercial for Motel 6 that ends with "We'll leave the light on for ya!" That promise leaves us with a warm feeling. We all need to know we are expected and wanted! We make so many mistakes and have so many regrets. We usually come to our senses if people give us enough time and love. When we hit bottom, we wonder if the light is still on. Does anyone still care? Will I be welcomed and received if I try to come back? It brings this poem to mind:

> Leave the light on!
> For kids who lose their way,
> For mates who go astray.
> Leave the light on!
> For friends who do you wrong
> And drain the music from your song,
> Leave the light on!

We'll Leave the Light On

For those who stumble and fall,
Who don't respond when you tearfully call,
Jesus keeps the light on for you!
So keep it shining for others too!

Thank God for those who leave the light on! Thank God for Suicide Hotline and for Call Rape! Thank God for the hotline for battered wives and for those who work tenderly and lovingly with scared, pregnant teens. They point them to people, places, and sometimes parents who have left the light on for them.

Thank God for those who see worth in rebellious teenagers and are anxious to give them a second chance. It's easy to denounce the rebel but hard to try to understand him and point him to a better way.

Thank God for churches that leave the light on. It's a shame so many don't. Stately buildings and lofty words don't compare to a naked light bulb, conveying, "We've been waiting up, hoping you'd call!" Churches must never lose sight of the message and ministry of reconciliation. We should heed the words of the old song by Phillip P. Bliss, "Let the Lower Lights Be Burning":

> Brightly beams our Father's mercy
> From His lighthouse evermore,
> But to us He gives the keeping
> Of the lights along the shore.
>
> Dark the night of sin has settled
> Loud the angry billows roar;
> Eager eyes are watching, longing
> For the lights along the shore.

Thank God for those who see worth in rebellious teenagers and are anxious to give them a second chance.

CHAPTER TWENTY-FIVE

Trim your feeble lamp, my brother!
Some poor sailor, tempest-tossed,
Trying now to make the harbor,
In the darkness may be lost.

Let the lower lights be burning,
Send a gleam across the wave!
Some poor fainting, struggling seaman
You may rescue, you may save.

The Tragedy of Waiting Too Long

Some slide so far into sin that they become callous (see Eph. 4:19). These include straying mates who wake up too late, sinners in the "someday" aisle, and those with eleventh-hour plans, who die at half past ten. No one knows what tomorrow holds, but today God's arms are outstretched. The Father is scanning the horizon, the church's door is open, and the light is on. Maybe you're sick and tired of being in the pigpen. At least the prodigal son knew where home was. He hoped the light would still be on, and he was so glad it was!

If you are wandering on the mountains of turmoil or in the valleys of despair, you should know that there's an open door, and his name is Jesus Christ. Maybe you've walked the path of sin too long. Make the trip home to God—home to his people and his church. You'll be so glad to find they've left the light on for you!